The Pocket Guide to Whisky

featuring the **WhiskyTubeMap**™

Blair Bowman
with Nikki Welch

BIRLINN

First published in 2017 by
Birlinn Limited
West Newington House
10 Newington Road
Edinburgh
EH9 1QS

www.birlinn.co.uk

Reprinted in 2018

ISBN 978 1 78027 432 4

British Library Cataloguing-in-Publication Data
A catalogue record for this book is available
from the British Library

Designed and typeset by Mark Blackadder
WhiskyTubeMap artwork by Go! Bang! Creative Ltd

Printed and bound by PNB Print Ltd, Latvia

Contents

Introduction

Growing up in Scotland it's hard to avoid whisky, it's everywhere. But the taste for it is not a given, I hated my first dram, which my dad gave me whilst camping (sorry Dad!). But the taste began to grow on me and I was curious to understand what all the fuss was about. When I arrived at Aberdeen University there wasn't a whisky society, so I decided to set one up with two post-grads. It was then that I started tasting a lot of different whiskies that I really began to develop an appreciation for the amber nectar.

Since then, my mission has been to show more people that there's a whisky out there for everyone, you just need to work out which one! I set up World Whisky Day to do this, celebrated annually on the third Saturday in May, which helps people around the world share some whisky love whether they are already whisky enthusiasts or new to whisky.

When I met Nikki and saw the WineTubeMap, and she told me she wanted to develop more flavour maps, I knew that it could work brilliantly for whisky, and that it would be a great way for people to explore whiskies so they could discover their own taste.

The rest, as they say, is history!

Slàinte Mhath!
Blair Bowman

How to use the WhiskyTubeMap

The WhiskyTubeMap is a flavour map of whisky, organising styles, types and specific brands from around the world by taste and texture rather than by geography. This makes it easy to navigate around the entire world of whisky just by knowing what you (or someone else) like. It is designed for everyone, 'frequent traveller' or complete beginner, to help explore and decode the sometimes daunting whiskies available.

Taste is a completely subjective experience and the WhiskyTubeMap helps you explore your own taste preferences rather than judging a whisky to be better or worse than another. All the whiskies on the map are good examples; what you like is down to you.

How it works

- O Each line has a flavour theme linking the whiskies together. The flavours evolve as the line progresses, generally running from light to intense.
- O Each station represents a whisky or type of whisky. They are divided into: Single malt; Blended whisky; Wood finishes and Types, and each stop will mention a whisky available in shops or bars. There is more information on how the stations are divided in the icons section on p. 7.
- O Some stations are intersections where multiple lines meet. These tend to be world classics because they represent a number of styles.

Public service announcement

It is impossible to include every whisky out there on the map, so this is an overall representation of whisky. Each station description in the book discusses other related whiskies and particular expressions to expand on this. (See Glossary on p. 139 for more information on expressions.)

How to use it

If you already know what you like:

○ Find your favourite whisky on the map; if it isn't there, check the index for extra whiskies, which will point you to the most similar starting station.

○ Try the stations that are closest to your favourite; these will be the most similar.

○ Continue to travel along the flavour line – if you reach a point that you are less fond of, head in another direction.

If you are feeling adventurous:

○ Find a whisky you know well on the map.

○ Head to the other end of the line that it is on for a more extreme version.

○ Or pick a completely different line and pick a whisky from there.

You may want to do this in a bar and try by 'dram' rather than paying for a new bottle every time!

If you are new to whisky:

○ Head to Starting Points, p. 10

If you are buying a gift:

○ Find out the lucky person's favourite whisky.

○ Select something from one of the surrounding stations.

For more suggestions head to the Advanced Manoeuvres chapter (p. 137) but most importantly, enjoy yourself.

Icons

To help you navigate the WhiskyTubeMap, each station has an icon which indicates the style of whisky at that station based on the production methods: Blended whisky, Single Malt whisky, Type of whisky (i.e. other production method or grain) or Wood Finished whisky. Many of them refer to specific distilleries or brands; others may be a description you will see on the label, like Port Wood Finish.

Public service announcement
When a station is a brand or distillery (e.g. Johnnie Walker or Jura) the description of the whisky is based on the prevailing house style of that whisky, and specific 'look out for' whisky recommendations are given as well. If you like the sound of a certain station but can't get hold of the recommended 'look out for' whisky, you won't be disappointed if you try other whiskies from that station/distillery.

 Blended whisky

The Blended Whisky icon refers, unsurprisingly, to whiskies made by blending a selection of different whiskies together, normally including both single malt whisky and single grain whisky. Single grain whisky usually makes up the bulk of a blend, as it is far cheaper to produce. This is then combined with various single malt whiskies, each adding their own unique flavour component. It is the job of a 'master blender' to create the recipe of whiskies that go into a specific blend, top-secret of course, and create one that tastes the same, batch after batch, and combines the 'best' elements of different styles of whisky into one smooth and easy-drinking dram. Whilst blends are often dismissed as being inferior to single malts, they hold a special place in the whisky industry, forming its backbone. Blended whisky is the basis on which Scotch whisky built its global reputation, thanks to the likes of Johnnie Walker and other grocers of the 1800s who created their own blends, which were then marketed to the world. It remains a key part of the international whisky economy: without it there would be no whisky industry.

Public service announcement

For the purpose of the WhiskyTubeMap, Monkey Shoulder, which is a blended malt, meaning a blend made solely from single malts, is indicated by the icons for both single malt whisky and blended whisky.

 Wood finish

The Wood Finish icon refers to whiskies that go through a 'finishing' process using a specific cask type to influence the ultimate flavour of the whisky. Most whiskies are matured in ex-bourbon or ex-sherry casks, or a combination of both. Some whiskies are then transferred to a different type of cask for a short while before being bottled, a process known as 'finishing'. At this point the whisky takes on more of the flavour of what was originally matured in the cask, for example, using a rum cask can give a whisky more coconut and tropical flavours, while a port cask gives a richer finish with some red-fruit flavours. Although any oak cask can be used to finish, there are a number that are regularly used and these are marked as stations on the map: Port Wood Finish, Sherry Wood Finish, Rum Wood Finish and Virgin Wood Finish (see the relevant stations for descriptions). Some distilleries, such as

Glenmorangie, produce a wide variety of finishes. However, the positioning of Glenmorangie on the WhiskyTubeMap is representative of the distillery's house style.

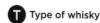

Type of whisky

There are a variety of different types of whisky based on their production methods and base ingredients, all of which can rightfully be called whisky or whiskey (US and Irish spelling), depending on where they come from. The whiskies/whiskeys within any particular 'Type' share certain flavours and textural similarities, and the stations on the map give you an idea of the overarching style of the type of whisky. Within each of the types of whisky there will be dozens of individual distilleries or brands making them. Classic examples of each type are given to help you navigate these stations.

Public service announcement

For the purpose of the *Pocket Guide to Whisky*, to avoid overuse of brackets the term 'whisky' replaces 'whisk(e)y' – the correct usage appears at specific stations.

Single malt

Single malt whiskies make up the majority of the stations on the WhiskyTubeMap. Single malt means whisky that is distilled at one distillery and made from malted barley, hence the name. As you will discover on the WhiskyTubeMap, single malt whisky can be made anywhere in the world, it is not just from Scotland. Despite being made in other countries the process and techniques are the same as in Scotland and most so-called 'New World' whiskies follow the rules and regulations associated with Scotch whisky. For the purpose of the WhiskyTubeMap the single malt stations are positioned based on their 'house style'; they may make more than one style of whisky, which will be highlighted in the station text.

Starting points

One of the hardest things about whisky is knowing where to start. It's all well and good if you've tried a few and have a good idea of what you do (or don't) like, but if you really aren't sure, even a WhiskyTubeMap can't help! Same goes for if you're buying a whisky as a gift or to take somewhere: if you don't know what your friends or hosts like it's a tricky call.

To help with this situation there are three specially selected Starting Point Stations on the map, identified by this icon ⌐. These stations are a good place to begin, if you don't know where to start.

Johnnie Walker (see p. 22 for more information)
A brilliant blended whisky which is a great starting point for anyone drinking whisky for the first time, or if you're trying to get over a bad whisky experience. Better still, it's readily available in pretty much every country, bar and supermarket in the world. An easy-drinking, smooth and not too in-your-face whisky to get you on the WhiskyTubeMap. Incredibly versatile if you don't feel like drinking neat whisky, it works brilliantly in cocktails or, especially well, with mixers.

Start here ...
... if you want something well balanced, smooth and easy-going.

Where next?
O After more of the same? Head north to Chivas and on to Bell's for more robust flavours.

- ○ Want something softer and more delicate? Head west to Famous Grouse and Dewar's.
- ○ Ready to taste something more complex and hit the single malts? Head south from Johnnie Walker to Benromach, Glenkinchie and Tamdhu, for a tour of fruity, sweet and easy-going single malts.

Glenfiddich (see p. 33 for more information)

A wise choice of starting place for anyone just getting started in whisky, or if you are returning to whisky after a long absence. For many, single malts are the epitome of Scotch whisky and this is a great introduction: it has won multiple awards and is readily available, with lots going on in the glass.

Start here ...

... to get started on single malts. It will help familiarise you with the flavours and style of a single malt but without being overly in-your-face or powerful.

Where next?

- ○ After more of the same? Head south to Glenlivet.
- ○ Similar but lighter? Head south-east to Glenrothes.
- ○ Something sweeter? Head north to Kentucky Straight Bourbon.

Highland Park (see p. 60 for more information)

A gateway whisky into the single malts which introduces the classic flavour of peat smoke. If the thought of a whiff of smoke in your whisky doesn't put you off and intrigues you, then Highland Park is a great starting point. The delicate smoke is balanced with a lovely sweetness.

Start here ...

... if you want to test your peat tolerance but don't want to go too far, too soon.

Where next?

- O After more of the same? Head east to Jura along the Coastal Line.
- O Want more peat and smoke? Head north to Bruichladdich on the ferry to the Outliers Line.
- O Want more sweet flavours? Head south over the footbridge to Macallan.

Public service announcement

Since some names are notoriously difficult to pronounce, we have included some guidance at each entry. Remember that 'ch' is pronounced as in the Scottish word 'loch' (i.e. with a softened 'ck' sound), not 'tch' as in 'sandwich' or 'k' as in 'lock'. So 'Glenfiddich' and 'Auchentoshan' both have the soft Scottish 'ch', which we have represented as 'c': Glen-fidd-ic.

Making the most of whisky

The WhiskyTubeMap has been designed to help you take the next steps on your whisky journey without all the whisky chat that can feel a bit stuffy. Whether you are buying a late-night dram, a bottle for home or a gift for someone, the rows of whisky in a shop or bar can feel daunting, particularly when the labels, packaging and unpronounceable names don't really give you a clue to the style or flavour of the whisky. By using the WhiskyTubeMap you can see how someone's favourite whiskies relate to other whiskies, making it easy to discover something new, which is great whether it is for yourself or when you are buying a gift for someone else.

The WhiskyTubeMap is here to guide you on a journey of flavour and discovery so you can explore the entire world of whisky. It's fun to know facts, trivia and history, but way more important than any of that is flavour. Probably the two most important things when deciding what whisky to try are your own taste preferences, and how much you have to spend.

For many, all whiskies seem to taste the same. Which is understandable, as whisky itself has a very distinctive flavour. However, line three whiskies up side by side, just for fun, and take your time tasting them: you'll be able to pick out differences in aroma, flavour and texture, even if you aren't a big whisky drinker. The more often you do this, the easier it will become and you will pick out things you do and don't like in a whisky, making it easier to explore.

Early experiences of whisky often involve shots of (inappropriately powerful or peaty) whiskies and so people are put off, not realising that there are more gentle whiskies out there. Once you start trying more whiskies you will soon start to learn what kinds of flavours you enjoy, which will help you navigate the next step in your journey.

How whisky is made
Certain things that happen in the process of making whisky can influence its flavour; know this, and you can start sifting one from another. Despite how it might seem, whisky-making is, in essence, a very simple process involving only three ingredients. Here's the process, in very simple terms, for a single malt whisky:

O Barley is soaked in water and then laid out on a floor for the barley to start to germinate.

O This germination is then stopped by gently heating and drying the barley (sometimes using peat smoke, if making a peaty whisky – see the Outliers Line p. 103).

O This is now malted barley, which is then mashed with warm water to form a kind of porridge-like mixture, the 'mash'.

O The liquid, known as 'wort', is drained off and yeast is added to it to create a beer-like alcohol, the 'wash'.

O The wash is then distilled to make 'new make spirit'.

O New make spirit is matured in oak casks (usually ex-bourbon or ex-sherry casks or a combination of both, to impart different flavours) for a number of years (minimum three years).

O The whisky is then bottled when it is considered ready. Once bottled the whisky will no longer mature, unlike wine. For more information see Storage section on p. 131.

This is, of course, an extreme simplification of the process. The maturation stage is where the magic happens and most of the final flavour of a whisky is determined. It is believed that the wood imparts around 70 per cent of the flavour. If you put an excellently made new make spirit into a poor cask you'll be left with a poor whisky. However, an average-quality new make spirit could be rescued by being put into a high-quality cask.

The three main influences on flavour are the grain used (single malt Scotch whisky is always made from malted barley, but other whiskies use different grains, like corn or rye); the way the grain is malted (with or without peat smoke); and the type of cask. If you can find this out, you can start to get a sense of what you like or dislike.

Use flavour to guide you, not age or colour

Does the age of a whisky matter? Is older whisky better? To put it bluntly, no, older whisky is not necessarily better. Remember that taste is a very subjective thing. For many years labelling a whisky with its age has been part of a marketing tactic to make aged whiskies seem more premium. Older whiskies do tend to be rarer, but that doesn't make them better. Older whisky spends more time in casks, so it can have more flavour from the wood and it often has more layers of flavour or complexity, making it a good whisky to take your time over. However, today there are an increasing number of whiskies without their age on the label and these can be just as delicious. Happily, these whiskies are helping to shift the dusty myth that 'older whisky is better'. What matters is flavour and what you like.

There is also a misconception that darker whiskies are better than lighter whiskies. Again, this is simply not true. The colour of a whisky is influenced by the type of cask it has been in. If it has been in an ex-bourbon cask it might be a light, golden straw colour. This type of cask will give the whisky lots of sweet vanilla and toffee notes, along with fresh woody and nutty notes. If a whisky has been matured in an ex-sherry cask it will be much darker, more of an amber colour, and this will give a whisky notes of dried fruits, dark chocolate, fruit cake and treacle. So remember: don't judge a whisky's quality by its colour.

Public service announcement

It is permitted for producers to add caramel colouring to a whisky. This might be done to darken a whisky or to maintain consistent colour.

Use occasion to help you decide how best to enjoy your whisky

Whisky drinking is most definitely a luxury (regardless of the price of the bottle). For this reason it should be enjoyed as such. The world, life and your own existence can happily survive without whisky, it just might not be as fun. As with wine, the sense of occasion plays an important role in the enjoyment of the luxury of whisky drinking. Getting home from work on a Friday night and wanting something easy drinking (see Easy Loop, p. 41), hosting a soirée and needing a wow cocktail to start the evening (see Cocktails, p. 122), or celebrating a special occasion, like a wedding, and needing a toast (see Decadent line, p. 63) are all great opportunities to reach for the whisky bottle.

Let the sense of occasion help you decide how you are going to drink the whisky. If it is more of a social event you might want it in a cocktail. Or if you want to learn more you might want to invest in whisky tasting glasses and plot a route of whiskies to try.

Let your nose do some of the work

What we call flavour is actually a result of our senses of smell and taste combining; the nose picks up the vast majority of the characteristics we detect and we combine that with the information we get from the tongue. So to get the most out of whisky it's useful to think about the aroma as well as the sensation when you're drinking the whisky. Your mouth can only experience the core tastes, like bitterness, sweetness and acidity, as well as the physical sensations of temperature, texture and the heat of the alcohol. Your nose does all the rest, from the TCP of peat, to honey, raisins or vanilla, which is why your nose is so important in the appreciation of whisky. In whisky tasting you 'nose' the whisky to get a sense of its flavours and style. Whisky blenders rarely taste a whisky until the final blends; most of the work they do is just by nosing the whiskies.

On top of this, our olfactory system (the technical term for the sense of smell) is intrinsically connected to our past memories and experiences. Our smell memory bank, or olfactory memory, helps us to recall certain smells or aromas but can also connect these to memories of experience too.

For example, when you smell oranges in a whisky you are in fact smelling the flavour and aroma compounds that combine to resemble that of an orange itself. Our sense of smell works as a whole and it's not easy for us to isolate individual smells or flavours; it is fun to try, and with practice it gets easier. Just don't worry if, at first, you don't manage to pick out individual smells, it takes time, which is a good excuse to keep trying new whiskies!

You can't see flavours or aromas and at first it can sometimes be difficult to translate these tastes and smells into words. It is like a radio presenter trying to describe a work of art to the listeners. The good news is that you don't have to put words to the flavour if you don't want to. Just experiencing them is very enjoyable.

Take your time to get the most out of your whisky

It's important to remember that we are talking about a drink here, so let's not be too precious about it. The most important thing when drinking a whisky is that you are enjoying it, be it with ice or water, with a mixer, in a cocktail (see Cocktails, p. 122 for suggestions) or simply neat, on its own.

The key to whisky on the rocks is using enough ice to prevent it melting too quickly: counter-intuitively, the more ice you add the less melt you get, as the ice keeps itself cold, which makes sense when you think about it. Whiskies on the Coastal line (p. 51) work well on the rocks because their strong flavours open up as the whisky dilutes. This is especially important if you are drinking a whisky with a mixer in a tall glass. Don't be stingy with two or three ice cubes, better the whole ice cube tray. You'll enjoy the drink right until the last drop, instead of having a melty, watery-tasting drink.

To add water or not …

Like everything, this is a case of personal preference. It is important to remember that drinking your whisky neat is not a sign of superiority! Water unlocks certain flavours in whisky, so adding a little water can give you a different experience. Most professional whisky-blenders water their whisky about 50:50 to get the full 'nose' from it. This is probably a bit too much for drinking, but adding a teaspoon or two of water will give you a real sense of the whisky. Remember, as well, that many 'cask-strength' whiskies are over 50 per cent alcohol, which means you may want to dilute the alcohol slightly to get past the burning sensation. It won't weaken the flavour at that strength!

Tasting or nosing?

Whether you have decided to drink your whisky neat, or with a splash of water, you can eke even more flavour out by taking your time to nose and taste it. A useful tool here is a good whisky nosing glass, to help you smell the complex aromas as they evaporate from the whisky. A nosing glass will help to concentrate the aromas so they don't dissipate too quickly.

Take your time nosing a whisky; your nose can detect much more than your taste buds ever can. Get your nose deep into the whisky and inhale gently. Try moving the glass between your nostrils to see if it changes what smells you detect.

When you are ready, take a sip. The second sip is normally where you can taste the most, as the first sip is really just waking up your palate to the alcohol. Let the whisky linger on your tongue, try to swirl it around your gums a bit to let it coat all the different parts of your tongue: you don't want to miss any of the important taste buds. Try to leave the whisky in your mouth for as long as you comfortably can before swallowing. Be mindful of this brief whisky-tasting moment. You will realise that this is much better than drinking whisky as a shot, where the moment is gone in an instant, and you also hardly taste any flavour except alcohol burn.

Most of all, enjoy it ...

Nosing, tasting, swirling, sipping will all enhance your whisky journey, but the most important thing to do is follow your own nose for what's right for you. So grab some friends and the WhiskyTubeMap and get exploring!

Johnnie Walker ◀

The Famous Grouse ⊛

Dewar's ⊛

Monkey Shoulder 🜂⊛

Auchentoshan 🜂

Hibiki ⊛

Virgin Wood Finish 🍶

Kentucky Straight Bourbon ⊤

Glenfiddich 🜂◀

Glenlivet 🜂

Single Grain Scotch Whisky ⊤

Single Pot Still Irish Whiskey ⊤

⊛ Blend   🍶 Wood finish   ⊤ Type   🜂 Single malt

◀ Starting point

1. Heart Line

The Heart Line cuts right through the varied whisky landscape of the WhiskyTubeMap, giving you a glimpse of what is in store. As you begin to explore you may wish to change lines to discover more. The line gets its name from distilling, the 'heart' of the distillation is the name given to the spirit that is held back and goes into casks to mature into whisky.

The journey contains some of the most well-known whiskies in the world alongside some wonderful world whiskies. It includes stops in Scotland, Japan, USA and Ireland, with whiskies varying from soft and delicate to spicy and fruity.

When to take the Heart Line

The Heart Line is diverse and will really help stretch your horizons. If you are ready to really start exploring the world of whisky then it is a great place to start, especially if you have been reluctant to try new things in the past. Any whisky bar worth their weight in barley would be a great place to explore the Heart Line.

Stations on the Heart Line

Johnnie Walker, The Famous Grouse, Dewar's, Monkey Shoulder, Auchentoshan, Hibiki, Virgin Wood Finish, Kentucky Straight Bourbon, Glenfiddich, Glenlivet, Single Grain Scotch Whisky and Single Pot Still Irish Whiskey.

Johnnie Walker

The biggest-selling Scotch whisky brand in the world. You can find a bottle of the 'striding man' in (almost) every single bar anywhere in the globe.

Pronunciation
As it looks.

What you need to know

○ An exceptionally well-balanced blended whisky. Johnnie Walker Red Label is sweet and delicate, it combines whiskies from across Scotland so is the epitome of blended whiskies. You will pick up hints of peat and honey as well as coastal whisky flavours within that overall sweet flavour.

○ A range of Johnnie Walker 'colours' are available to discover, including blends featuring old and rare whiskies as well as blends made of smokier whiskies. Try Johnnie Walker Double Black if you fancy the smokier style.

○ It is one of the most iconic and global whiskies, sold in 200 countries, and that's not a new thing. In 1920 Johnnie Walker whiskies were being sold in around 120 countries.

Best enjoyed ...
In a hotel bar when visiting a new city in a foreign country. The taste will be familiar and comforting, especially if you are experiencing a bit of a culture shock. If you are in a particularly hot climate, why not have a Johnnie Walker Black Label on the rocks? Or if you fancy something cooler, then go for a Johnnie Walker Red Label with ginger ale and lots of ice. Feeling flash? Then try a Johnnie Walker Blue Label neat.

Setting the scene

Imagine being transported on a whistle-stop tour of Scotland's distilleries, all combining together to make the whisky in your glass. Johnnie Walker is a blended whisky, sometimes consisting of over 40 different single malt and single grain whiskies. The precise recipe is a closely guarded secret. The blends are always of an exceptionally high standard and complement each other. If you are looking for a Scotch whisky that fits all circumstances and environments, then have a Johnnie Walker.

Bar chat

○ There are four flagship Johnnie Walker Houses in Beijing, Shanghai, Chengdu and Seoul. These are described as luxury embassies for Scotch whisky. Unfortunately, they are invite-only. You'll need to befriend some 'guì bīn' (Chinese for VIP) in order to get in.

○ Look out for Johnnie Walker Blue Label: this is the most premium of the colour range and is rich and velvety with hints of ginger and orange, and a subtle smoky layer.

The Famous Grouse

The best-selling whisky in Scotland since 1980, this classic dram is a favourite at Christmas time and is epitomised by the feisty game bird – forever linked to the start of the game-shooting season in Scotland. It has long been associated with rugby in Scotland due to their sponsorship of the national rugby team for several years.

Pronunciation

As it looks.

What you need to know

- An easy-drinking and richly flavoured blended whisky which is fruity and zesty, a bit of a Goldilocks, not too heavy, not too light, not too sweet, not too dry.
- Like many blended whiskies The Famous Grouse pulls together whiskies with different styles to create a harmony of flavours. Famously they use Highland Park for its fresh, coastal flavours and Macallan to add a bit of sweet rich flavour, amongst others.
- Originally known as 'The Grouse' it was rebranded in 1905 on the 12th August, also known as 'the glorious twelfth' (the name given to the start of the grouse shooting season) and became 'The Famous Grouse'.

Best enjoyed ...

From a hip flask watching a rugby match; it is probably rainy and cold, but the warmth of The Famous Grouse will cheer your spirits whether your team win or lose.

Setting the scene

The Famous Grouse Experience at Glenturret Distillery in Perthshire is the so-called 'spiritual home' of this blended whisky. Set on the banks of the River Turret, the distillery has records dating back to 1775 and claims to be the oldest distillery in Scotland, a claim contested by a handful of others. A popular tourist destination, the visitors' centre receives around 80,000 visitors a year.

Bar chat

- The Famous Grouse adverts have been on TV for over thirty years, with a very distinctive jingle, 'all together now!'.
- Look out for The Famous Grouse Smoky Black edition, a lovely smoky alternative featuring peated malt whisky from Glenturret as part of the blend.

Dewar's

The most awarded blended Scotch whisky in the world, and the best-selling blended whisky in the USA.

Pronunciation
Due-Arrs (not Doo-Arrs)

What you need to know
○ A very easy-to-drink blend with distinctive honey and heathery notes.
○ Dewar's blended whisky is made from around 40 different single malt whiskies combined with grain whiskies. Aberfeldy whisky is always at the 'heart' of any Dewar's blend, giving it its honeyed tones.
○ Dewar's works wonderfully over ice or as a base in classic cocktails (see Cocktails, p. 122), both of which enhance the aromatic quality of the whisky.

Best enjoyed ...
On the rocks or with a splash of water. However, the balance of sweet honey and soft heather notes works beautifully in any cocktail.

Setting the scene
Take a tour of the Highlands by travelling the length of the A9. This road is the gateway to the Highlands, with several distilleries dotted along the route. Dewar's whisky is blended from up to 40 different whiskies; see how many you can 'bag' on your journey.

Bar chat
○ *It's Scotch!* from 1898, a short advert for Dewar's whisky, was the first ever motion picture advertisement.

O Stick to Dewar's White Label for your drinks cabinet as the base of your cocktails.

Monkey Shoulder

A major intersection on the WhiskyTubeMap, where blends and single malts collide in an über-cool blended malt.

Pronunciation
As it looks.

What you need to know
O Monkey Shoulder is a sweet but not too sweet whisky with orangey, citrus notes.
O This whisky is a blended malt whisky which differs from the traditional blended whiskies in that the blend consists only of single malt whiskies. Monkey Shoulder is made from Glenfiddich, Balvenie and Kinninvie.
O Monkey Shoulder is a funny-sounding name for a whisky, but it is in fact named after a medical condition that sometimes affected maltmen, the men who turned malting barley by hand, who would develop this type of repetitive strain injury, a bit like 'tennis elbow'.

Best enjoyed ...
In an Old Fashioned cocktail (p. 124). The great thing about this whisky is its versatility. It has been specifically designed to work well in cocktails but also works fine on its own.

Setting the scene
Take a stroll in a new city you've never been to before, think Prague, Tokyo, Melbourne or Miami. Go into the coolest new cocktail bar in that city (do some online research before you

go), ask the bartender what their favourite Monkey Shoulder cocktail is and you'll be guaranteed to get a unique treat.

Bar chat

O Thanks to a specifically 'disruptive' approach to marketing, this brand has become a favourite of bartenders around the world. The Monkey Shoulder team have created the world's first telescopic bar spoon, so you can carry it in your pocket. Most recently they reintroduced a forgotten type of cocktail shaker that spins on handles called the 'konga' shaker, which is as fun as it sounds!

O Look out for any bottle of Monkey Shoulder. They only make one expression so if you find one, you've found them all.

Auchentoshan

A classic, light Lowland whisky from the outskirts of Glasgow. This whisky has a fresh and delicate taste and as a result has been affectionately dubbed a 'breakfast whisky' (please drink responsibly).

Pronunciation:
Oc-En-Tosh-An

What you need to know

O Whiskies from Auchentoshan all have a delightful softness to them, in part due to the special distillation process used, but it is not so soft as to lose any flavour. Aromas of rich dried fruits and sweet caramel chocolates are most prevalent.

O Auchentoshan's triple distillation technique is pretty unique among Scotland's distilleries; the others distil their whisky twice. The extra process brings the spirit up to a higher strength, which removes more of the volatile compounds, making it lighter and fresher tasting.

O The Lowland region was once a hub for distilleries, due to its proximity to Glasgow and Edinburgh. Auchentoshan is one of only a handful of distilleries in the Lowland region but several new distilleries are planned.

Best enjoyed ...

With a half pint of lager – to be truly authentic, order Tennant's (the biggest-selling lager in Scotland). This is known as a 'hauf and a hauf' in Scots (a half and a half), as you have a glass of whisky and a half pint of beer, as a chaser for the whisky.

Setting the scene

If you get to Glasgow, spend the day visiting the distillery, it's not far from the city centre. Then that evening head to the Pot Still or Bon Accord bars (or better yet, both) to get a really authentic experience of drinking in two of the best whisky bars in Glasgow. Remember to order a 'hauf and a hauf'.

Bar chat

O Production stopped during World War II. In March 1941, the main road running past the distillery was made, using various lights and props, to resemble the River Clyde, in order to divert the German bombers from bombing the Clyde shipbuilders and the docks. The decoy river worked, but unfortunately several warehouses were destroyed by the bombing and over 1 million litres of whisky were lost as a result. The distillery was repaired in 1949.

O Look out for Auchentoshan Three Wood, so-called for being a combination of whiskies matured in ex-Bourbon, Oloroso sherry and Pedro Ximenez sherry casks, which gives it a well-rounded and rich flavour.

Hibiki

A gateway into Japanese whisky and onto the Intrepid Line. Hibiki is a delicious blended whisky from Japan.

Pronunciation:
Heh-Bee-Kee

What you need to know

- A well balanced and sumptuous whisky with sweet fruits and a delicate softness to it. There is also a slight waxiness and oakiness in the palate.
- This blended whisky includes single malt whisky from Yamazaki (p. 69) and Hakushu (p. 80) (both stations on the WhiskyTubeMap in their own right) as well as grain whisky from Chita Distillery, which makes it a good Japanese whisky to cut your teeth on.
- Japan is getting a name for its whisky production, many of which regularly win awards. It is also the third largest producer of whisky in the world, with first place going to Scotland and the US in second.

Best enjoyed ...
As a highball in a busy Japanese whisky bar. A highball is the name given to any drink that has an alcohol base and a non-alcoholic mixer. However in this context it means Hibiki whisky and soda water over ice. Get large ice cubes in your glass then add one part Hibiki whisky to two parts soda water, stir and enjoy. This spritzy and fresh way of enjoying whisky is almost too easy to drink.

Setting the scene
Take the Bullet train to the countryside and enjoy the wonderful views. If you time it right and go in late March you may be lucky

enough to see the wonderful Japanese cherry blossoms in full bloom.

Bar chat
- O Unlike Scottish distilleries who trade barrels with rival brands in order to produce blended whisky, Japanese distilleries are fiercely competitive and keep their whiskies to themselves.
- O Look out for the aptly named Hibiki Harmony, a wonderfully elegant and well balanced whisky.

Virgin Wood Finish

Virgin Wood Finished whiskies are a relatively recent addition to the whisky family, and a great way to step from bourbon into Scotch.

What you need to know
- O Whether a whisky is matured completely or just for the finishing stage in virgin wood, you will find barrel-loads of toasty oak notes, unsurprisingly, but also plenty of sweet vanilla notes from the fresh wood as well.
- O Virgin wood (not a sacrificial wood ritual) refers to oak barrels that have not previously held anything and that are 'fresh'.
- O Virgin Wood Finish is still pretty controversial and new. Scotch whisky producers have long had a ready supply of ex-bourbon barrels (which by US law can only be used once for maturing bourbon), so it has not been necessary to experiment with virgin wood, which many producers believed overpowered the flavours in Scotch whisky.
- O There are relatively few Scotch whiskies that have been entirely matured in virgin oak; however, it is often used as a

'finishing' process. This means that the whisky is matured in virgin oak for a short amount of time before it is bottled, to impart an extra boost of oak and vanilla aromas.

Best enjoyed ...

Late in the day, perhaps as a pre-dinner aperitif. These whiskies are often quite zingy and spritely but with handfuls of tropical fruits and nuts thrown in too. There will also be plenty of vanilla sweetness, and this would work equally well after dinner with a crème brûlée.

Setting the scene

Immerse yourself in virgin wood in the forests of the Ozark Mountains, where giant oak trees stretch out high into the sky above you. These forests cover an area over 24,000 square miles and stretch across the states of Arkansas, Missouri and Oklahoma. It is not unusual for some of the trees to be between eighty and a hundred and twenty years old. Ultimately, these trees will become barrels.

Bar chat

O The topic of virgin oak finishing has become quite divisive within the whisky industry, with some companies wholeheartedly endorsing it while others are sticking to their guns and not jumping on the bandwagon.

O Look out for Auchentoshan Virgin Oak, it is deliciously fresh with orange and spices, plus a lovely sharp finish.

Kentucky Straight Bourbon

Dive into a world of creamy vanilla and spiced honey notes as you set off on a road trip of the Bluegrass State's finest whiskey.

What you need to know

- 90 per cent of all US bourbon is made in Kentucky and is characterised as being rich and woody as well as lip-smackingly sweet whiskey.
- Bourbon can only be made in the USA and is officially 'America's Native Spirit'. Kentucky Straight Bourbon is a distinct style of bourbon that has been made in Kentucky following even stricter guidelines than bourbon.
- Kentucky Straight Bourbon must be made from a minimum of 51 per cent corn, which gives it its sweet flavour (with rye, malted barley or wheat making up the rest), and aged for a minimum of two years in new-charred oak barrels. No colour or flavouring may be added to Straight Bourbon; the only thing that can be added is water before bottling.

Best enjoyed ...

On a blisteringly hot day in an American dive bar with no air-conditioning. Ask the barman what his favourite Kentucky Straight Bourbon is and order a large measure on the rocks.

Setting the scene

Head to Louisville, Kentucky on the first Saturday in May for the Kentucky Derby, an annual horse race. It's going to be hot, so cool off with a Mint Julep (see p. 125), the official cocktail of the Kentucky Derby. Over the two race-day weekends some 120,000 Mint Juleps are consumed each year, using nearly 500 kg of mint leaves in total!

Bar chat

O Sometimes a part of the mash (the mix of corn plus other grains) from the most recent distillation is added to create consistency across batches; this is known as a sour mash.

O A 1968 directive from the United States Bureau of Alcohol, Tobacco, Firearms and Explosives defines the official spelling as 'whisky' in the USA. However it allows labelling as 'whiskey' to respect tradition. So, let's stick to tradition and call it whiskey.

O Look out for Bulleit Bourbon, a spicy, peppery, vanilla-sweet whiskey. Other good examples are Wild Turkey, Woodford Reserve and Buffalo Trace.

Glenfiddich

Glenfiddich is part of the foundations of single malt whisky, a perfect starting point onto the WhiskyTubeMap and where the Amber Line meets the Heart Line.

Pronunciation:
Glen-Fidd-Ic

What you need to know

O Whiskies from Glenfiddich are all very drinkable and their core range offers subtle but interesting variations of flavour and aroma. The 'house style' will give you lots of light and fresh fruit notes.

O Glenfiddich is one of the lighter styles of single malt, priding itself on its fresh flavours. These are combined with a mix of barrels from both bourbon and sherry to give the finish a rounded flavour that isn't dominated by one or the other.

O Until recently Glenfiddich was the number one-selling single malt whisky in the world but don't let that put you off. Large-scale production doesn't always mean it's not well made.

Best enjoyed ...

On a celebratory weekend away at a boutique country house hotel. After dinner sink into one of the plush sofas in the library. Instead of petit fours ask for a Glenfiddich with a frozen slice of pear (yes, you read that correctly!) in the glass. Although this isn't a classic serve it's a great, refreshing way to enjoy a late-night whisky. You never know, you might start a trend.

Setting the scene

Head to Dufftown, in the heart of Speyside, also known as the 'malt whisky capital of the world'. There is a saying that goes 'Rome was built on seven hills, Dufftown stands on seven stills', however there are now only six working distilleries. Take a few hours for a walk around the town and 'bag' them all. Remember to leave time to visit the Whisky Shop Dufftown, on the High Street, whose shelves are full to bursting, so fill your boots and bags with bottles to take home.

Bar chat

O Pioneers in all senses of the word, in the 1960s Glenfiddich were the first distillery to promote single malt whiskies internationally. Prior to this, nearly all whisky was sold as blended whisky.

O Look out for Glenfiddich 15-year-old, an impressively rich and spicy whisky, which is also exceptionally smooth and sweet. Using a take on the Solera system, more commonly used to age sherry, this whisky is made from a vatting of 15-year-old whisky that is left to 'marry' in a large tun. Whenever whisky is taken out new whisky is added. So at any time there is a mix of new and old whisky, which is then bottled.

Glenlivet

One of the busiest intersections on the WhiskyTubeMap. From here you can travel on almost any flavour route desired.

Pronunciation
Glen-Liv-It

What you need to know

O The Glenlivet is full of floral and grassy green notes, along with plenty of fruitiness.

O The single malt that 'started it all'. George Smith, who owned Glenlivet, was the first legal distiller in the Highlands. The parish of Glenlivet was at the epicentre of illicit distilling and smuggling routes.

O Surrounded by other illicit distillers and smugglers in the area who were outraged that George Smith would run his distillery legally, he famously had to carry two hair-trigger pistols with him at all times for protection.

O Despite completing a major expansion of the distillery in 2010, Glenlivet is undergoing further expansions to potentially triple its capacity and maintain its position of being the biggest-selling single malt Scotch whisky in the world.

Best enjoyed ...
At home, give yourself some space, turn off the TV, get rid of any distractions and get comfy. Take a deep breath and relax. Have a sip and savour the flavours on your tongue, you've earned this!

Setting the scene
The Glenlivet Distillery lies on the edge of the Cairngorms National Park. A beautiful part of Scotland, you can see Munros

(Scottish mountains over 3000 feet) stretching far into the distance. As you stand in the glen you can imagine the old days of smugglers scurrying around the hills. Let the history and sense of place wash over you, then take in a tour of the recently modernised distillery while thinking back to how it all began here.

Bar chat

O In the late 1800s the quality of Glenlivet whisky was so highly regarded that many other distilleries, even those nowhere near Glenlivet, started to add the name Glenlivet to their brands as an indication of quality.

O Look out for Glenlivet 15-year-old. This whisky has been partly aged in French oak casks, which impart a soft and sweet nuttiness as well as delicate spice.

Single Grain Scotch Whisky

A hugely under-appreciated style of whisky. Single grain is the backbone of blended whisky but stands up well on its own too. Without blended whisky, and hence without single grain whisky, there really wouldn't be a whisky industry in Scotland.

What you need to know

O Due to the continuous distillation process, single grain whiskies are very light-tasting, with lots of pear drop and citrus notes.

O Grain whisky differs from single malt whisky, because it is made using a continuous distillation process (which is used in vodka, white rum and other white spirit production). This process makes a lighter and fresher spirit and is much cheaper and faster to produce than malt whisky. It is made using some malted barley along with other unmalted cereals, usually corn/maize or wheat.

O It has the unfortunate reputation of being rough-tasting but if it has been in good-quality casks or is of a considerably older age (think twenty years plus), single grain whiskies can be a refreshingly different alternative to a fine single malt.

Best enjoyed ...

Next time the sun is out, go and find a bottle of single grain whisky, preferably an older cask-strength one, and stick it in your freezer overnight (don't worry, it won't freeze because of the alcohol). Then as the sun sets the following evening, pour yourself a glass of your super chilled grain whisky, preferably into a large wine glass. The viscosity will be thick and syrupy, because it has been in the freezer. The first few sips may make you think you are drinking a crisp white wine. Watch the sun set, and as the whisky adjusts back up to normal temperature more and more flavours will be revealed. Simply divine.

Setting the scene

Unlike single malt distilleries, which can often be very picturesque, single grain distilleries are very much industrial-sized factories that are not so easy on the eye. Furthermore, they are not open to the public. So just enjoy your grain whisky at home in your back garden.

Bar chat

O There are only seven grain distilleries in Scotland. Until very recently, single grain whisky was simply not marketed, only a handful of independent bottlers would sell it.

O In 2014, in conjunction with Diageo, David Beckham launched a new brand of single grain Scotch whisky called Haig Club.

O Look out for Girvan Patent Still, a fresh and floral single grain whisky and independent or single cask bottlings. They make a welcome change from single malt whisky.

Single Pot Still Irish Whiskey

Currently in the midst of a renaissance, single pot still Irish whiskey is a juicy, fruity and spicy cousin of single malt Scotch whisky.

What you need to know

- Single pot still Irish whiskey always has a spicy and peppery character because of the green malt used in its production. But don't be put off by all that heat, it's balanced with sweeter apple and raisin flavours too.
- It can only be made in Ireland, contains a mix of malted and unmalted barley (known as green malt) and it is triple distilled. The green malt gives it its spicy flavour and the triple distillation produces a smoother, lighter spirit, making it quite unique.
- Until 2011, single pot still Irish whiskey was labelled as 'pure pot still whiskey', so if you see a bottle labelled as this you know it's going to be old-school.

Best enjoyed ...

In Ireland in a bar that is so full of people that they are spilling out onto the road. With a folk band in the corner drowning out the buzz of the chatter with bodhran (drum), accordion and fiddle. When you eventually get to the bar don't order a Guinness, you'll end up spilling it if someone bumps into you in the rammy, get a large glass of single pot still Irish whiskey and just soak up the atmosphere.

Setting the scene

Take a trip to Midleton Distillery, the godfather of the Irish single pot still whiskey's renaissance. This distillery currently produces the following brands: Redbreast, Yellow Spot, Green Spot and the eponymous Midleton, all of which are stunning examples of single pot still Irish whiskey.

Bar chat

○ You can also get single malt Irish whiskey, which is made using only malted barley.

○ Look out for Redbreast 15-year-old, a rich, fruity and spicy treat. Christmas cake is often used to describe whiskies, so it sounds a bit cliched and even lazy, but this is exactly that – Christmas cake distilled.

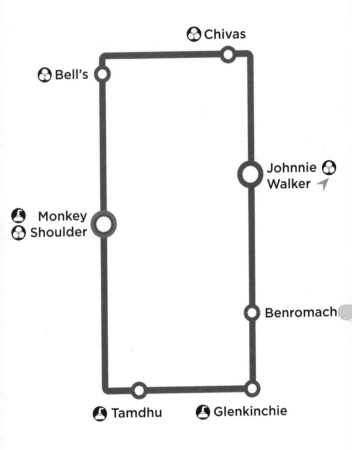

Chivas ⊗

Bell's ⊗

Johnnie ⊗
Walker ↗

⊗ **Monkey**
⊗ **Shoulder**

Benromach

Tamdhu ⊗   ⊗ **Glenkinchie**

⊗ Blend   ⊟ Wood finish   🅣 Type   ⊗ Single malt

↗ Starting point

2. Easy Loop

The Easy Loop does exactly what it says on the tin. These whiskies are easy-going and will appeal to all tastes. If you are just embarking on your whisky journey then this loop is an ideal place to start. You will discover blended whiskies as well as getting a chance to dabble your tastebuds in some laid-back and tasty single malts.

If you depart to the north of Johnnie Walker on the Easy Loop you will explore more from the world of blended whisky. If after Johnnie Walker you are ready to get stuck into single malts then depart to the south. Head west to join the Heart Line, which will take you through the heart of the WhiskyTubeMap.

When to take the Easy Loop
If you need to take a whisky to a party or want to offer an after-dinner dram to guests, you won't go wrong with these. Alternatively, if you have had a long day at work and you want something to sip on that isn't too complex but with plenty of flavour, then again you can't go wrong with these drams.

After work, after dinner or after whenever, these will work.

Stations on the Easy Loop
Johnnie Walker, Bell's, Chivas, Monkey Shoulder, Tamdhu, Glenkinchie and Benromach.

Johnnie Walker

See the Heart Line p. 22.

Chivas

Although a blended Scotch whisky, Chivas is better known over the pond or in the nightclubs of Asia.

Pronunciation
She-Vass

What you need to know
- This whisky is creamy, with hints of vanilla and dried fruits, like bread and butter pudding with custard.
- As with most blends, the whiskies used come from across Scotland, however Chivas pride themselves on having a 'Speyside' accent, which translates as a creamy, sweet characteristic.
- Chivas is the second largest-selling whisky in the world behind Johnnie Walker, but it predates Johnnie Walker as the world's first luxury blended Scotch whisky: Chivas Regal 25-year-old was launched in the USA in 1909.

Best enjoyed …
In the VIP area of a super-chic nightclub with friends. Forget the champagne, order a bottle of Chivas and share it with your friends. Get some mixers for those who want them or ice if it's hot in the club.

Setting the scene

If you want to visit a picture-postcard distillery then head to Strathisla, the 'spiritual home' and a major malt whisky component of the Chivas blend. Drive north from Aberdeen and you'll be there in an hour. With its traditional pagoda roofs and a water wheel, it's hard to find a prettier looking distillery.

Bar chat

O Like many blends, Chivas can trace its origins to a grocery store, this one at 13 King Street in Aberdeen, where it was first made. More recently this address was a Chinese restaurant and is now the offices of a dementia charity. A small plaque on the wall outside commemorates the original grocery store.

O Look out for Chivas 18-year-old. A sumptuous and warming whisky with lovely chocolatey notes as well as a delicate floral nose.

Bell's

Part of the north branch of the Easy Loop, Bell's is the best-selling whisky in the UK, a classic dram that has been favoured for generations.

Pronunciation

As it looks.

What you need to know

O A mellow and fruity blend with very subtle hints of smoke. Think fruit cake with glacé cherries and smoked almonds.

O Bell's uses Blair Atholl single malt at the base of its blends, which gives it the classic fruit cake and almonds flavour. It is then combined with a range of other whiskies to create the

Bell's recipe, so you'll get a hint of all the other whisky flavours, including a waft of smoke.

O For thirty years Bell's have been producing commemorative bell-shaped decanters to mark various events, such as royal weddings and the like. Despite being marketed as collectors' items, all of these have been produced in large numbers.

Best enjoyed ...

'Afore ye go' has been the strapline for Bell's since 1925, so why don't you have this as a final dram before you leave for your next adventure, whisky or otherwise, or in other words, have one for the road.

Setting the scene

The brand home for Bell's is Blair Atholl Distillery as it is a major component of the blend, in the town of the same name, set in the beautiful Perthshire hills. If you visit you must leave plenty of time for a visit to Blair Castle, which is also where the Keepers of the Quaich, a prestigious society that recognises individuals who evangelise Scotch whisky, hold their banquets twice a year. On the way home stop for tea and scones at House of Bruar, where you can pick up everything from plus fours to smoked salmon.

Bar chat

O If you have happened to inherit a Bell's decanter from a relative or you find one in your granny's attic you may be disappointed to hear that they are not worth a huge amount. A recent auction lot of twenty-two Bell's decanters from 1988 up to 2009 sold for only £250. You might be better just opening it and enjoying it, as it is probably what your granny would have wanted!

O Look out for Bell's Original, a nutty, slightly spicy blended whisky. It is the only whisky with the Bell's label, apart from the odd commemorative decanter.

Monkey Shoulder

See the Heart Line p. 26.

Tamdhu

A slightly under-the-radar single malt, but a hidden gem.

Pronunciation
Tam-Doo

What you need to know
- An easy-drinking whisky full of vanilla, toffee-fudge and sweet, red fruit flavours.
- The whiskies from Tamdhu are 100 per cent matured in sherry casks, imparting a lovely rich fruitiness.
- Until the new owners took over in 2013, Tamdhu had been rarely seen as a single malt in its own right, as the whisky was all earmarked for blends, such as The Famous Grouse.

Best enjoyed ...
On a luxurious train ride, think the Orient Express or the Royal Scotsman trains. Take in the scenery as your country house on wheels rolls smoothly through the landscape, be it Alpine mountains or Scottish glens. This easy-drinking and full of flavour whisky will make the hours slip away in a most enjoyable way.

Setting the scene
The former Knockando railway station and waiting room sit adjacent to the distillery and there are plans to turn them into a visitors' centre in the future. For now hop on the Keith to

Dufftown railway, known as 'The Whisky Line'; you'll ride in old 1950s carriages. Keep an eye out the windows and count how many distilleries you can spot, the ones with traditional pagodas are a useful giveaway.

Bar chat

O Built in 1897, the distillery was designed by Charles C. Doig, Esq., the most distinguished distillery architect of the day. It was described as being the most modern and efficient of its time.

O Look out for Tamdhu 10-year-old: the bottle is distinctive and stands out on a back bar full of whisky bottles.

Glenkinchie

Known as 'The Edinburgh Malt' due to its location, the whisky from here is soft and delicate.

Pronunciation
Glen-Kintch-Ee

What you need to know

O A very soft and fragrant whisky, with hints of flowers and grass plus an additional nutty maltiness.

O Glenkinchie is one of only a handful of distilleries in the Lowlands. Its delicate floral and fresh fruit notes are typical of classic Lowland whiskies.

O It is currently the nearest distillery to the city of Edinburgh, which makes it perfect for a day trip (however, there are plans for a new city-centre distillery in the pipeline).

Best enjoyed ...
After watching the Royal Edinburgh Military Tattoo at Edinburgh Castle. After the performance head down the Royal Mile from the Castle, and when your feet get tired stop in the nearest pub and order a dram of Glenkinchie. Having just listened to over 100 minutes of massed pipes and drums, you'll probably be feeling your inner Scotsman coming out as you sip and savour the light and fruity dram.

Setting the scene
You would be crazy not to visit Edinburgh as part of a whisky pilgrimage. Sidestep the tartan whisky bars and go to Devil's Advocate, Usquabae, Scotch at the Balmoral and the Scotch Malt Whisky Society. These are some seriously impressive whisky bars that you will wish you could take back home with you.

Bar chat
O Look out for the Glenkinchie Distillers Editions: the most recent is a wonderful example of an Amontillado sherry-finished Glenkinchie with lovely sherried, fruity notes.

Benromach

A great single malt if you are a fan of blends. A delicious whisky that makes you wish you had discovered it sooner. It is truly a classic Speyside dram.

Pronunciation
Ben-Ro-Mac

What you need to know

- Whisky from Benromach is expertly crafted, with a great deal of emphasis put on the quality of casks used. You will find classic malty, grassy, gingery spice and sherry notes in these whiskies.
- Benromach use a mixture of bourbon and sherry casks like many other distilleries, but they often finish their whisky in newer Oloroso sherry casks to get that final, sweet sherry note.
- The distillery was founded in 1898. Over the years the business changed hands regularly but it was acquired by independent bottler Gordon & Macphail in 1993. Gordon & Macphail have sourced, bottled and blended whiskies in the traditional way at their premises on South Street, in Elgin, since 1885. They are one of only a handful of businesses in the whisky industry that is still family-owned and -operated.

Best enjoyed ...
After a long, snowy countryside walk at Christmas time. As you warm up by the fireplace take a nice long sip of this whisky, and really chew it to get the flavours dancing. You'll warm up inside and out.

Setting the scene

Forres is a delightful town on the Moray Firth and apparently has its own microclimate. Only 25 minutes from Inverness by train, the town also plays host to the European Pipe Band Championships each year. After visiting Benromach Distillery get back on the train and head to Elgin (only another 15 minutes by train) and visit the Gordon & Macphail shop (owners of Benromach Distillery) on South Street. They currently stock over 1000 different whiskies.

Bar chat

O Look out for Benromach 10-year-old, an excellently smooth and juicy whisky. With a wonderful chewy mouth feel, this is an easy-drinking dram that packs serious flavour.

Glenlivet

Oban

Springbank

Scapa

Old Pulteney

Jura

Highland Park

 Blend   Wood finish   **T** Type   Single malt

 Starting point    Foot path   Ferry line

3. Coastal Line

The Coastal Line is a seafaring voyage in flavours. Set forth and you will encounter the salty, briny taste of the sea, but don't be put off as these are balanced with delicate, floral and fruity aromas too.

Heading westward from Glenlivet you will begin to notice more maritime influences in these whiskies as you gradually approach the sea at Highland Park.

When to take the Coastal Line
If you've already done a bit of exploring around the Whisky-TubeMap and feel ready to get stuck into some whiskies that are a bit more robust and punchy, then this is the perfect place for you to journey next. This line leads to the gateway of the peaty island flavours of the Outlier Line, so it's a great journey if you're not yet ready for the full-on peat effect. Coastal Line whiskies need time to develop in your glass, so don't rush it; they also tend to work really well with cheese, so gather some pals together, put on a cheeseboard and take your time as you explore the line.

Stations on the Coastal Line
Glenlivet, Oban, Springbank, Scapa, Old Pulteney, Jura and Highland Park.

Glenlivet

See the Heart Line p. 35.

Oban

Oban Distillery lies a few minutes from the harbour, nestled in the bustling resort town of the same name. The town is known as the 'Seafood capital of Scotland' due to its busy harbour bringing in boatloads of langoustines, lobster and North Sea fish, as well as being the gateway to the Western Isles.

Pronunciation
Oh-Bun

What you need to know
- O The whiskies from Oban have lovely wisps of salty peat smoke and a gentle, sweet yet drying gingery note as well. You will find some hints of seaweed and sea spray too, but this shouldn't be so strong that it is off-putting.
- O They say the sea flavours come from the fact that the distillery's worm tubs (see Glossary p. 139 for more information) are exposed to the salty sea air all year round.
- O The distillery is right in the centre of the busy little town and surprisingly dates back to before the town, which sprang up around the distillery.

Best enjoyed ...
On board the MV *Hebridean Princess*, a luxurious little 72-metre cruise ship – it's like a private yacht-cum-floating country house. You set sail from Oban Harbour towards the Western Isles. As the sun sets you sip a dram of Oban as you stand on the deck watching the town disappear over the horizon.

Setting the scene

The town sees an influx of around 25,000 visitors during the height of the season, but don't let this put you off. Oban is a wonderful place to stop for a night or two before taking a CalMac ferry and visiting the islands of the Inner and Outer Hebrides. Oban lies on the Gulf Stream, so it's not your typical rugged and weatherbeaten seaside town. After visiting the distillery grab an ice cream and mosey around the harbour soaking up any exceedingly rare Scottish sunshine (available on certain days of May, June and September).

Bar chat

- ⭕ The word Oban in Scottish Gaelic means 'the little bay'.
- ⭕ Look out for the eponymous Oban Little Bay, a lovely whisky with hints of black pepper and ginger as well as peaches and apples.

Springbank

A whisky with a cult following, and for good reason. Springbank is renowned for its uncompromising quality and attention to detail, avoiding any of the tricks of the trade to ensure the whisky is always made according to tradition.

Pronunciation

As it looks.

What you need to know

- ⭕ Springbank is a complex whisky, which is quite lightly peated but exceptionally rich and fruity. It is a classic maritime- and coastal-tasting whisky.
- ⭕ The unique flavour is partly thanks to its unusual two-and-a-half times distillation process, but also down to the

distillery's exacting quality-control process. It is renowned for never chill-filtering or adding caramel colouring. It also bottles many single cask whiskies.

○ Springbank is the oldest independent family-owned distillery still in production in Scotland. The whole production process, including bottling, labelling and packing, happens on site at the distillery, a fact it is proud of. It is a major employer in the remote town of Campbeltown.

Best enjoyed ...

With a very close friend. A dram of Springbank is to be sipped and savoured. However, like any whisky, it tastes better when it's shared. Choose a good friend, one who you know won't down the glass of whisky as soon as you hand it to them, and enjoy the excuse to hang out together.

Setting the scene

Towards the southern tip of the remote Kintyre peninsula lies the fishing town of Campbeltown. After visiting Springbank Distillery, no visit to Campbeltown would be complete without visiting Wm Cadenhead's Whisky Shop and bottling your own single cask whisky direct from the cask. Then head over to the award-winning whisky bar at the Ardshiel Hotel, where you will be spoilt for choice by their list of over 700 whiskies and rare bottlings.

Bar chat

○ Campbeltown was once a hub of whisky production, with nearly 30 distilleries in operation; sadly only three active distilleries remain there. In the nineteenth century it was known as the 'whisky capital of the world'. Despite the dramatic decline in distilleries in the area it is still recognised as a 'protected locality'.

- Look out for Springbank 15-year-old, a top-notch whisky that has a full spectrum of flavours from nutty and chocolatey notes to dried fruits and vanilla. If you smoke cigars then this would be a wonderful dram to have with a prime Cuban.
- As well as producing Springbank, the distillery also produces two even more distinctive single malts, namely: Hazelburn (triple distilled) and Longrow (which as a heavily peated whisky would sit on the Outlier Line). These are definitely worth looking out for too.

Scapa

The somewhat lesser-known single malt from Mainland, Orkney. This whisky is unpeated but still has a delicate island and coastal charm to it.

Pronunciation
Ska-Pa

What you need to know
- Scapa can be elusive and hard to get your hands on as it is not widely available as a single malt. When you do bag your Scapa you will find it particularly smooth for an island malt: it has a delicious creamy texture with subtle notes of tropical fruits and melon.
- Scapa's unique flavour is created by a pair of 'Lomond' wash-stills. It is the only distillery to still use these; the shape means the spirit produced is particularly rich and smooth. Combine this with solely American first-fill barrels and you get the distinctive Scapa smoothness.
- The distillery was sadly mothballed in 1994 and lay dormant for ten years until 2004, when the distillery was completely renovated and started producing whisky again. During the

closure, staff from Highland Park (see p. 60), the other distillery in Orkney, would make whisky at Scapa for a few months each year, just to help keep stock levels up.

Best enjoyed ...
On a sunny day sitting on the grassy verge outside the distillery, looking over the beautiful bay of Scapa Flow, from where the distillery takes its name. Or if you're not actually on an island, pop your feet in a paddling pool and recreate the moment in your garden.

Setting the scene
Orkney is a magical place to visit. The 70 islands that make up the Orkney Islands also have a strong connection with the Vikings and Norse history, and you can feel the past as you stand at the end of the British Isles looking north to Shetland and beyond. It's easy to imagine prehistoric life here; the islands have incredible examples of Neolithic standing stones at the Ring of Brodgar, and archeologists are continuing to discover Stone Age sites and towns dating back some 800 years before Stonehenge. The food in Orkney is also of a very high quality and definitely worth trying if you love seafood. For visiting whisky fanatics you get a double whammy at Orkney's Mainland island, as you can visit both Scapa and Highland Park.

Bar chat
O During World War I, Navy officers were lodging at Scapa Distillery when a fire started. The Grand Fleet, anchored in Scapa Flow, quickly sent men ashore. Using a human chain to carry buckets of water they managed to save the distillery from burning down.

O Look out for Scapa Skiren, a smooth and tropical dram with lots of lemon and pear notes. Also, keep your eyes peeled for the now-discontinued Scapa 16-year-old, a remarkable creamy, vanilla, honeyed dram.

Old Pulteney

Old Pulteney is affectionately known as the 'Maritime Malt', and for good reason, as you will see when you come to taste it.

Pronunciation
Old-Pult-Nay

What you need to know

O You will get just a faint wisp of a smoky sea breeze from Old Pulteney, as it is virtually unpeated. However, there are still plenty of other maritime notes such as briny seaweed and old, waxy ropes.

O The copper pot stills at Old Pulteney are unique, with very large 'boil balls' which have inspired the shape of the Old Pulteney bottles. The unusually large boil balls add to reflux during distillation, creating a lighter spirit.

O Wick was at one time known as the herring capital of Europe and it is likely that whisky was, at that time, aged in herring barrels. You could mature whisky in herring barrels, but for obvious reasons distilleries don't do this any longer.

Best enjoyed ...
With a sea salt-rimmed glass (like when you have a margarita). To do this, run fresh water round half of the lip of a whisky tumbler then dip the wet rim in sea salt flakes. Try taking some sips from the salted edge and some sips from the unsalted edge. See how the salt and whisky mingle on your tongue and change the taste experience in your mouth.

Setting the scene
This is a great distillery to visit if you are doing the Proclaimers-inspired 500-mile road trip (aka the North Coast 500), which runs from Inverness round the north coast of Scotland with

stunning scenery. Scotland has no law of trespass, so if you hire a camper-van you can just park up and camp under the stars after you've hiked the hills and glens as you come across them. Stop off at the distillery in Wick, 100 miles north of the start point in Inverness, to pick up a bottle or two to accompany you on your jaunts. After a visit to the distillery head to the well-stocked whisky bar at Mackay's Hotel in the centre of Wick. Bizarrely, the entrance to the hotel's restaurant happens to be on the shortest street in the world, Ebenezer Place, stretching a total of 2.06 metres.

Bar chat

- ○ Until recently Old Pulteney was the most northerly mainland distillery in Scotland (usurped by Wolfburn Distillery in Thurso in 2013).
- ○ Look out for Old Pulteney 12-year-old, a lovely, sweet, sherried and maritime dram.

Jura

Only ten minutes by boat from Islay, the isle of Jura has only one road, one pub and one distillery on it and is home to more sheep than humans, with fewer than 200 inhabitants living on the island.

Pronunciation
Joo-Rah

What you need to know

- ○ A softly peated whisky, unlike its pungent neighbours from Islay. Whisky from Jura is very easy-drinking and sweet with just the odd briny note.

- Jura is one of the few distilleries to produce a full range of expressions, ranging from light and fresh to peaty and heavy. The description is for the original style; if you like that, you can experiment with some of the other expressions, which might take you onto a completely new line!
- The island has very distinctive mountains that dominate the skyline of the whole area, the highest being over 2500 feet. These mountains are known as the 'Paps of Jura' due to their steep sides and conical shape ('pap' is the Scots word for breast). They can be seen from mainland Scotland and Ireland on a clear day.

Best enjoyed ...

After an arduous journey to the Isle of Jura (see below for explanation). Dump your bags, collapse into a chair, and pour yourself a large dram of Jura, you've arrived at last. This is the moment you have been waiting for. There is a beautiful Scottish Gaelic word that describes this sensation perfectly: *sgriob* (pronounced skree-up), meaning the itchiness that overcomes the lip before taking a sip of whisky.

Setting the scene

Jura is famed for being very difficult to get to. George Orwell wrote *1984* while on the island and described it as the most 'un-get-at-able place'. The simplest way to get to Jura would be to fly to Islay from Glasgow Airport and then get the ten-minute ferry crossing to Jura. The other option is to drive from Glasgow to Kennacraig (two and a half hours) on the Kintyre peninsula, then get the ferry to Port Askaig on Islay (two hours) then change to the Jura ferry. All in all, a long and fairly complicated trip. But once you get there a dram of Jura will certainly make it worth all the effort.

Bar chat

O The islanders of Jura are supposedly very superstitious. Jura superstition is a lightly peated version of Jura whisky: tradition dictates that you should not cut peat before May. This whisky uses exactly that – pre-May-cut peat!

O Look out for Jura Origin, a brilliant everyday dram, lots of sweet flavours and not overly complex. If you are after something a bit peatier, try Jura Superstition.

Highland Park

Highland Park is a bustling intersection on the WhiskyTubeMap. The end of the Coastal Line, from here you can take the ferry to the Outlier islands or walk over the footbridge to the Decadent Line.

Pronunciation
As it looks.

What you need to know

O Highland Park whiskies are almost exclusively matured in sherry casks, giving the whisky a lovely sweet fruit and nut aroma which combines with the delicate peat smoke to create a unique sweet and smoky palate.

O Highland Park is situated on Mainland, Orkney and is one of the few remaining distilleries to continue to malt its own barley. Locally cut peat is used, which differs quite significantly from the peat found on Islay, being heathery and aromatic.

O Just over a mile as the crow flies from Orkney's 'other' distillery Scapa, Highland Park has a loyal global fanbase of people who love it for its soft, fragrant, peat-smoke and fruity, sherry and heathery honey notes. Orcadians (people from Orkney) are proud of Highland Park, and rightly so.

Best enjoyed ...

It is not uncommon to encounter a storm on Orkney, where a dram of Highland Park by a roaring fire is the perfect antidote. Recreate this moment at home when the rain is pouring down and you are cosy and warm inside, and rather than bemoaning the rain, remember the famous saying 'rain is whisky waiting to be made'.

Setting the scene

Because of its location and small population there is very little light pollution on Orkney, making it the perfect place to see the Northern Lights in the winter months. The best place by far is one of the most northerly islands that make up Orkney, Papa Westray. From Kirkwall (on Mainland, Orkney) head to the island of Westray and board the Loganair flight to Papa Westray – it is the shortest commercial flight in the world. Officially scheduled to take just two minutes, including taxiing, the flight can take under one minute on a good day. Certainly not enough time for an in-flight dram.

Bar chat

O Because of Orkney's connection to the Vikings, Highland Park is exceedingly popular in Scandinavia, so much so that many Highland Park aficionados there even have the logo tattooed on their arms.

O Magnus Eunson, credited with establishing the distillery at Highland Park, was a preacher by day and a whisky smuggler by night. Rumour has it that he would hide illicit whisky under the pulpit in the church. Which should mean you'll always be forgiven if you've been a bit naughty by drinking Highland Park (DISCLAIMER: this is not a guarantee).

O Look out for Highland Park 21-year-old. A complex dram with soft, sweet smoke but plenty of rich flavours of orange peel and strong dark chocolate.

Glenlivet

Glenmorangie

Kavalan

Balvenie

Yamazaki

Amrut

Port Wood Finish

Macallan

Sherry Wood Finish

 Blend   Wood finish   Type   Single malt

Foot path

4. Decadent Line

Welcome to the world of luxury whiskies. These rich, opulent whiskies are ones to take your time over: the more you sip and savour, the more layers of flavour you will find. Like a luxury car or watch, these are well-crafted, sumptuous and a bit indulgent, but they still do the job! You won't find any rough edges on the Decadent Line, just silky-smooth, rich whiskies to wallow in. No need for private jets here, the Decadent Line takes you on a tour of Scotland, Taiwan, Japan and India, with short stops in Spain and Portugal for the all-important sherry and port casks.

When to take the Decadent Line
When you are feeling like you want to do something a bit special or raise a dram in celebration. Or maybe you have tasted a lot of great everyday drams and you are now looking for something more complex to get stuck into. Particularly good to sink into at the end of the night for some reflective conversation.

Stations on the Decadent Line
Glenlivet, Glenmorangie, Kavalan, Balvenie, Yamazaki, Amrut, Port Wood Finish, Macallan and Sherry Wood Finish.

Glenlivet

See the Heart Line p. 35.

Glenmorangie

Pioneers of finishing whisky in different types of cask, Glenmorangie has been the biggest-selling single malt whisky in Scotland since the early 1980s.

Pronunciation
Glen-Morrun-Jee (stress the 'mor' and rhyme with orangey)

What you need to know
O A deliciously smooth and velvety whisky. Glenmorangie offers up lots of well-balanced and harmonious flavours of orange and chocolate, with fresh malty and dried fruit notes too.

O The whiskies are made using the tallest copper pot stills in Scotland. The stills are 8 metres tall (26 feet ¼ inch), which is roughly the same height as an adult giraffe. This creates a very light and delicate spirit.

O Glenmorangie was the first distillery to really experiment with using casks from different types of wine and fortified wine to affect the ultimate style of the whisky. Unlike some distilleries, who use their casks several times, Glenmorangie only uses casks twice, in order to get the most flavour from the wood during maturation.

Best enjoyed ...
On a comfy leather sofa in the middle of a Highland glen. This image may ring a bell, as it was used in a late '90s advertising campaign for Glenmorangie.

Setting the scene

Just under an hour by car from Inverness, north on the North Coast 500, the distillery sits on the banks of the Dornoch Firth. After a tour of the distillery head down to the beautiful secluded beach at Portmahomack (twenty minutes by car). A leisurely walk along the sandy beach head is well rewarded by dinner at The Oyster Catcher (a restaurant with rooms). After dinner try a few drams from their extensive 'Malt Vault'.

Bar chat

O Glenmorangie owns a large area of forest in the Ozark mountains in Missouri. The felled American white oak is then air dried before being made into so-called 'designer casks'. These casks first go to bourbon distilleries to mature before going to Glenmorangie.

O Look out for Glenmorangie Signet, a luxuriously smooth and rich whisky. It's like a melt-in-your-mouth chocolate pudding, with lots of notes of green apple and honeyed citrus. Simply divine!

Kavalan

The Taiwanese have a huge thirst for Scotch whisky but are now producing their own fantastic award-winning single malt whisky in Taiwan too at the first whisky distillery in the country.

Pronunciation

Ka-Va-Lan

What you need to know

O A smooth, tropical-tasting whisky, with lots of pineapple and mango flavours.

- Due to the warm and humid subtropical climate in Taiwan the whisky matures more rapidly than in Scotland. This gives the whisky a more tropical, rich flavour and means the wood influence is more intense sooner than it would be in a Scotch whisky.
- Founded in 2005, Kavalan has taken the whisky world by storm. Initially it faced several sceptics but these were quickly appeased once they tasted the product and realised just how good it was.

Best enjoyed ...
In an air-conditioned room on a hot and humid day. Drink ice-cold mineral water between each sip of whisky to cool your palate as it warms to the tropical notes of this whisky.

Setting the scene
Although Taipei, capital of Taiwan, might not be top of your travel bucket list, you may find yourself on a stopover to somewhere else with time to kill. If you have time, you could escape the metropolis and be at the King Car Distillery, where Kavalan is made, in an hour, and if you need a bit of nature after all that tasting, the orchid gardens next door will provide a feast for your eyes.

Bar chat
- In 2010, Kavalan was in the headlines in the UK after coming out top in a blind taste test against three Scotch whiskies. The event was organised by *The Times* newspaper, and the results 'shocked' the panel of judges.
- Look out for Kavalan Classic, a smooth, light-tasting whisky with lots of tropical fruits and dried mango notes. Also keep an eye out for their single cask 'Solist' releases; they are exceptional.

Balvenie

Despite being neighbours, and sharing the same water source, Balvenie and Glenfiddich are distinctly different whiskies. Balvenie is the sweeter and more honeyed whisky of the two.

Pronunciation
Bal-Ven-Ee

What you need to know
- A cracking Speyside dram. A wonderfully soft and sweet whisky with lots of honey flavour and delicate wood spices.
- Balvenie is one of only a handful of distilleries that still operate their own floor maltings. They are able to malt up to 15 per cent of the barley that goes into making Balvenie. They add a very small amount of local peat, which you get the faintest whiff of in the whiskies.
- Built in 1892 by William Grant, owner of Glenfiddich, the Balvenie and Glenfiddich distilleries are next door to one another in Dufftown.

Best enjoyed ...
On a starry night in the ruins of Balvenie Castle. The Balvenie Distillery stands in the shadow of Balvenie Castle, which was originally built in the twelfth century but was ultimately abandoned in the 1700s. If you don't happen to have a castle to hand, this is the perfect whisky to pop into a hip flask and take camping with you. Drink with friends to warm you up as you watch the stars.

Setting the scene
Balvenie only opened to the public recently but it is definitely worth pre-booking a tour if you plan to visit. They only run a limited number of tours per day and keep the size of the group

very small. After a visit to the distillery, why not walk back in to Dufftown and get a whisky ice cream at the Balvenie Street Ice Cream Shop? Then take a seat next to the Dufftown Clock Tower, the point where the main roads of Dufftown meet, and watch the world go by, including dozens and dozens of lorries carrying malted barley and/or whisky to and from the distilleries.

Bar chat

O Balvenie is also one of only a few distillers to have on-site coopers. This ancient craft of barrel-making is normally outsourced, but Balvenie is preserving it and recently, controversially, moved its coopers to be salaried rather than the traditional way of paying piecemeal, per barrel (which was believed to make them work faster, but potentially more prone to error).

O Look out for Balvenie DoubleWood. A classic dram from Balvenie that really shows the true 'house' style of Balvenie. First launched in the early '90s, this whisky is initially matured in an American oak bourbon cask and then finished in a European oak sherry cask, hence the name 'doublewood'. There are lots of fruity, sherry notes in this dram and it is very drinkable.

Yamazaki

Yamazaki was the first whisky distillery built in Japan and continues to be the biggest-selling single malt there. It is now getting harder than ever to find this highly regarded Japanese single malt.

Pronunciation
Yam-A-Zack-Ee

What you need to know

- Yamazaki whiskies are intensely rich and fruity with a great depth of flavour to them. Lots of dried fruit flavours like prunes and plums, with nutty and sweet toffee notes too.
- Although most Japanese whiskies use bourbon and sherry casks, unlike the rest of the whisky world they also use Japanese oak (mizunara) to finish the whisky in. This enhances the sweet vanilla and toffee flavours.
- Yamazaki Distillery was built in 1923 by Shinjiro Torii, the founder of Suntory, but Yamazaki was not marketed as a single malt until the release of Yamazaki 12-year-old in 1984. Prior to this the whisky was going to blends. Due to the surge in demand for Japanese single malt whisky, Yamazaki is immensely popular.

Best enjoyed ...
As a Mizuwari (literally: 'mixed with water'), a very popular way of drinking whisky in Japan. As with tea ceremonies, Japanese culture and tradition dictates that there is a set ritual to follow when making a Mizuwari. First fill a long glass with ice and pour in one part Yamazaki. Stir thirteen and a half times. Add more ice and add two parts still mineral water. Stir three and a half times. Enjoy.

Setting the scene

If you are heading to Tokyo and looking for an excuse to take the famous Bullet train, you could do worse than head to the Yamazaki Distillery by taking the train to Kyoto. Or if you can't make it to the distillery join the after-work crowd in one of the many urban whisky bars. These bars are tiny, pristine celebrations of whisky. They are always presided over by a 'master' bartender who serves and creates with flourish and ceremony.

Bar chat

O Masataka Taketsuru is credited with being the founding father of Japanese whisky. In the 1920s he studied at Glasgow University, did apprenticeships in Scottish distilleries and then took the knowledge back to Japan.

O Look out for Yamazaki Distiller's Reserve, a fruity and rich whisky with hints of spices and perfume. A proportion of this whisky has been matured in mizunara casks. Also keep an eye out for Yamazaki 18-year-old, an incredibly elusive but spectacular whisky.

Amrut

Made in Bangalore, India, Amrut was the first Indian single malt whisky to take the whisky world by storm.

Pronunciation

Am-Root

What you need to know

O Amrut's whisky tastes surprisingly mature despite being quite young in age. It has lots of woody and sweet milk chocolate notes as well as dried fruits. It could be mistaken for some classic Speyside single malt whiskies.

O Due to the high temperature, as well as the altitude of the distillery (3000 feet) the whisky matures rapidly. The angels' share can be up to 15 per cent volume (lucky angels!). It has been estimated by Amrut that one year maturing in India is equal to roughly three years in Scotland. This intensifies the flavours and wood influence. The final product is hugely influenced by this unique climate to make whisky in.

O There are many spirits in India called whisky which aren't made in the traditional way. Amrut's owners decided that they wanted to make a high-quality single malt whisky made following the same process as would happen in Scotland.

Best enjoyed ...
With someone who, snobbishly, would turn their nose up at the idea of an Indian-made single malt. Give them a dram of Amrut but don't tell them what it is right away. They will quite quickly tell you they enjoy it, at this point mention that it's an Indian single malt and watch the surprise on their face!

Setting the scene
It is hard to think of a place that feels further away from the peace and tranquillity of the Highlands of Scotland. Imagine, instead, making whisky amongst the hustle and bustle, heat and humidity of a contemporary Indian city, full of traffic, people, exciting smells and tastes. Welcome to the world of Indian single malt whisky.

Bar chat
O Most so-called Indian whisky isn't whisky as we know it, because it is made from molasses. Amrut and Paul John, another Indian single malt whisky, are so important because they make their whisky using malted barley the 'proper' way.

- A lot of Indians would love to be buying Scotch whisky but the 150 per cent import tariff makes it prohibitive and they are forced to buy local whiskies instead.
- Look out for Amrut Fusion, a whisky distilled using barley from India and a portion of peated, malted barley from Scotland. These are distilled and matured separately at first then 'married' together for about six months before bottling. This whisky is very malty and oaky, with lots of sweet orange and marmalade notes to it.

Port Wood Finish

Ruby-coloured and bursting with red-fruit flavours, Port Wood Finished whiskies put a deliciously different character in your glass.

What you need to know
- Port Wood Finished whiskies will give you a veritable fruit salad of red-fruit aromas and flavours. Think strawberries, raspberries, red currants, cranberries and cherries.
- Traditionally, whisky is matured in American oak casks that have been used for bourbon. With port casks, the whisky takes on fewer vanilla, sweet notes and more complex berry notes as well as adding a distinctive ruby-red tint to the whisky.
- Some distilleries will have an ongoing relationship with some of the most renowned port houses; most of the latter won't add their name to the label, but the success of the style means that this is changing. Expect to see some of the big-name whiskies and port houses hooking up publicly in the future.

Best enjoyed ...

When you are after a whisky but looking for something a bit different that will give you more fruitiness. If you can't decide whether you want a soft, sweet whisky or a robust, strong whisky then go for a Port Wood Finished to combine the best of both.

Setting the scene

Head to Porto to soak up some of the local atmosphere. Visit the waterfront where the port warehouses sit on the riverbank, take a boat along the River Douro to see the port vineyards and enjoy a leisurely lunch in one of Europe's hidden gems of a city break. If you can't make it there console yourself with a *pastel de nata* (custard tart) and a nip of Port Wood Finish whisky at home.

Bar chat

- A Port Pipe is the name given to the type of cask that the port wine industry use. These casks are typically 650 litres and have a distinctive tapered end.
- Look out for classic examples of Port Wood Finish: Balvenie 21-year-old Port Wood, Glenmorangie Quinta Ruban, Glen Moray Classic Port Cask, Tomintoul 15-year-old Port Finish, Arran Port Cask Finish and Talisker Port Ruighe.

Macallan

Nearly the end of the Decadent Line and only a short walk to get you to the Coastal Line. Macallan is one of the most highly regarded and sought-after single malts in the world, in terms of both quality and prestige.

Pronunciation
Mack-Allan

What you need to know

O The Macallan is famed for being a predominantly sherried whisky. It is smooth and rich with lots of raisin, sweet toffee and honey notes.

O The Macallan Distillery has 'curiously small' stills that help to produce a distinctively heavy, oily new make spirit which adds to the richness of the whiskies.

O A huge amount of effort goes into making Macallan whisky, particularly in the way the signature sherry casks are managed and used.

O Before the 1980s the Macallan was a hardly known brand, but in high demand from whisky blenders because of its rich, sweet flavour. Thanks to substantial marketing budgets and promotion it quickly became a stalwart of hotel bars and luxury venues around the world.

Best enjoyed ...

By creating a ceremonial atmosphere. Like the moment where the party stops for the popping of a champagne cork, take your time over the foil and stopper and listen for the squeak of the cork. Once you've let the genie out of the bottle there's no going back ... Unlike champagne, you can then pass the bottle around as a symbol of friendship and good times.

Setting the scene

If you're heading to Speyside, no trip is complete without a mini pub crawl on the doorstep of Macallan. And you can't get any more different than these three whisky stops: the world-famous Quaich Bar in the Craigellachie Hotel, an A-lister hang-out (if it's good enough for Kate Moss ...); the Highlander, an old-school Highland hotel with whisky, tartan and haggis aplenty; and finally the Fiddichside Inn. Joe, the proprietor, is eighty-seven years old and has been pulling pints and serving drams in the pub for almost sixty years. You will instantly be made to feel like a local in his pub, it is a true institution.

Bar chat

- The 'new' Macallan distillery will open in early 2017, after a major expansion and modernisation of the distillery and visitors' centre costing £100 million.
- Look out for the Macallan Gold (note this has replaced the Macallan 10-year-old fine oak in certain markets), quite a citrussy Macallan with lots of lemons and oranges as well as classic sherry notes.

Sherry Wood Finish

The end of the Decadent Line and the whisky to finish your night on. If you have a sweeter tooth you will love getting stuck into these wonderfully rich, deep, fruity, sherried whiskies.

What you need to know

- Sherry-matured whiskies are almost impossible to resist. Generally they have more of an amber hue to them and a lot of dried fruit notes and aromas, which makes them slightly sweeter and softer than some other styles. Some of these whiskies can take on so much of the sherry character that it's hard to tell whether you are drinking heavily fortified sherry or heavily sherry-matured whisky.

O The most intense sherry character comes when the whisky is solely matured in sherry butts, for a more subtle effect the distillery may combine sherry- and bourbon-matured elements together. These whiskies can sometimes be a bit more expensive, due to the fact that an ex-sherry butt is approximately ten times more expensive than an ex-bourbon barrel.

O Until now the term 'sherry' has been used generically, however, some distilleries are now specifying on the label which type of sherry was previously in the cask. Most tend to use oloroso, but look out for PX and the others in future.

Best enjoyed ...
At midnight. This is definitely the dram to pour when you fancy a late nightcap or you're feeling reflective. It's the kind of whisky you can tease out until you're ready to go to bed or until the sun rises. You don't need a lot of it to get the full experience.

Setting the scene
Sherry is having a renaissance and the best place to get a feel for it is Jerez on the south coast of Spain. There you can spend the day visiting sherry bodegas and the night feasting on tapas and drinking lots of sherry, but remember, nothing really happens until 11 p.m., so pace yourself. Once you've got the bug you'll be delighted to find sherry bars popping up in Edinburgh, London and around the country so you can still get your sherry fix.

Bar chat
O Whiskies at this station are often referred to as 'Sherry Bombs' by whisky aficionados.

O The sherry industry has suffered over recent generations and reduced its production, which has resulted in fewer sherry casks being available to the whisky industry. As a result, many sherry casks are simply built at cooperages in Spain and then 'seasoned' with sherry for a short time. It is much harder for distilleries to source ex-sherry butts that have been used to age sherry.

O Look out for these classic examples: Aberlour A'bundh, Glenfarclas 105, Glendronach 21-year-old Parliament, Benriach 17-year-old PX sherry finish, Dalmore Cigar Malt Reserve and Mortlach Special Strength.

Monkey Shoulder

Hakushu

Mackmyra

Hibiki

Rye Whiskey

Teeling

Sullivans Cove

 Blend   Wood finish   Type   Single malt

Ferry line

5. Intrepid Line

To boldly go where your palate has never gone before. The Intrepid Line is full of robust and vibrant whiskies. A journey that travels from Scotland to Japan, Sweden, America, Canada, Ireland and Australia. A brave new world of whisky awaits.

When to take the Intrepid Line
When you are feeling experimental and want to expand your whisky repertoire beyond single malt Scotch. It is also highly useful if you need to impress or surprise a whisky buff. The Intrepid Line challenges even the most die-hard Scotch traditionalist to open their mind.

Stations on the Intrepid Line
Monkey Shoulder, Hakushu, Mackmyra, Hibiki, Rye Whiskey, Teeling and Sullivans Cove.

Monkey Shoulder

See the Heart Line p. 26.

Hakushu

Hakushu is a Japanese single malt both intrepid and bold that acts as a gateway to peatier whiskies on the Outlier island. It is a lovely fresh, crisp Japanese whisky with just a hint of smoke.

Pronunciation
Hah-Koo-Shoe

What you need to know

○ Whisky from Hakushu is distinctly different from many other Japanese whiskies in that it is much lighter and fresher-tasting, and also has a subtle amount of smokiness to it.

○ The distillery is found in a mountain forest and is one of the highest whisky distilleries in the world. The pure water and altitude both factor in the fresh, pure style. Although the style is fresh, Hakushu whiskies carry a subtle smokiness. They create a lightly peated spirit as well as a heavily peated spirit. Once matured these two whiskies are sometimes blended together to create a balance of peat and smoke.

○ Hakushu is owned by Suntory, who also own Yamazaki Distillery. Hakushu is their second distillery and was built fifty years after Yamazaki.

Best enjoyed ...

With a large ice ball. Japanese bartenders are obsessed with high-quality, crystal-clear ice. This dates back to the days when ice was a luxury commodity only available to the nobility in Japan. A Japanese bartender can expertly craft a perfectly spherical ice ball from a large block of ice in a matter of minutes, it is a real art. They will carve the ice ball to be as large as possible to fit in the glass and no more. The size of the ice ball means that the dilution of the whisky will be very gradual. The aesthetic beauty of this ritualistic serve is strongly connected to the Japanese philosophy of wabi-sabi.

Setting the scene

You would be forgiven for thinking that Japan was all 'Hello Kitty' and *Lost in Translation*. But step away from the hustle and bustle of Tokyo and you can find a world of solitude, hills, scenery and clean air, just like the Scottish Highlands. The Hakushu Distillery is set in the lusciously green forest foothills of Mount Kai-Komagatake, in the southern Japanese Alps just three hours from Tokyo, so a visit there is a good excuse to get out into the gentler side of Japanese life.

Bar chat

○ Parent company Beam Suntory also have major business interests in Scottish and American whisky distilling. They own iconic US whiskey brands such as Jim Beam and Maker's Mark as well two famous Islay distilleries, Bowmore and Laphroaig.

○ Look out for Hakushu Distiller's Reserve, which features lots of green fruits, herbaceous notes and just a hint of smoke.

Mackmyra

The first whisky distillery in Sweden opened its doors in 1999 and is now well-established as a must-have on the whisky map, as well as being a symbol of a new age of whisky making.

Pronunciation
Mack-Mee-Rah

What you need to know

O Mackmyra whiskies are strong flavoured and generally bottled at 46 per cent abv or higher. You can expect lots of woody notes, fiery spiciness and green herby notes, but these will vary depending on the expression.

O Mackmyra whiskies are distinctive: their barley tends to be sweeter because of the warmer summers, giving the whiskies a toffeed edge and the woody, spicy notes are due to the Swedish oak barrels. Swedish oak grows in a harsher climate than American or mainland European oak and so the grain is rougher, which means it imparts a more robust flavour.

O You'd be forgiven for not knowing about Swedish whisky, it's a new thing! In 1998, a group of friends on a skiing holiday asked the question: 'why is there no whisky made in Sweden?' A year later that same group of friends made their first drops of whisky at Mackmyra. In 2011, their new Gravity Distillery opened. The production process innovatively relies heavily on gravity, and in doing so uses 45 per cent less energy than more conventional methods.

Best enjoyed ...
After skiing a run that you are particularly proud of! Mackmyra tastes unique and with strong, punchy flavours is not for the faint-hearted. It represents a challenge to the status quo and

demonstrates what happens when you come out of your comfort zone, so is the perfect celebration for a brave day's skiing.

Setting the scene
Stockholm makes a great destination for a weekend city break. You can feast your eyes on seriously stylish Scandi restaurants or on the Swedish street food, smorgasbords, and immerse yourself in the watery, outdoorsy Swedish lifestyle by cruising around the archipelago and immersing yourself in the 'hygge' culture. A visit to the Gravity Distillery at Mackmyra Whisky Village about two hours north of Stockholm by car is a lesson in the Scandinavian approach to eco-driven, aesthetically pleasing design (and there's more delicious food there too).

Bar chat
O Look out for Mackmyra Svensk Ek (Swedish oak) matured in Swedish oak casks. This whisky is spicy, woody, peppery, gingery and has hints of mintiness. Keep an eye out for their distinctive branding and bottles, you can't miss them.

Hibiki

See the Heart Line p. 29.

Rye Whiskey

The original pre-Prohibition spirit and the base of some of the most classic cocktails that originated in this era across America.

Pronunciation
As it looks.

What you need to know
- In the US, rye whiskey differs from bourbon in that it must be made from a minimum of 51 per cent rye, by law, which gives it a distinctive flavour. It has more spiciness and is less sweet than bourbon.
- The remainder of the rye whiskey is distilled with a mixture of barley, wheat and corn, some use more rye and some less, more rye equals more spice, whilst more corn adds sweetness.
- If an American rye whiskey is aged in new oak casks for a minimum of two years it can be called a 'straight rye whiskey'. Straight rye whiskey tends to have a sweeter edge than other rye whiskeys.
- Confusingly, Canadian whisky is often referred to as rye whisky, or simply rye, because it has a strong history of being made from rye. However, the laws do not state how much must be used so it doesn't necessarily taste the same.

Best enjoyed ...
In a classic cocktail while channelling your inner Don Draper. Fix yourself a Manhattan, an Old Fashioned or a Sazerac (see Cocktails, p. 122). These classics are dry, and strong, meaning you have to strike a pose and sip slowly; too many and there will be a Draper-esque meltdown!

Setting the scene

Still channelling your spiritual Don Draper, get yourself to America and into a rustic-looking dive bar. Now follow these steps: 1) Loosen your tie (if you happen to be wearing one). 2) Run your hand through your hair, to obtain that dishevelled post-long-day-at-the-office look. 3) Shout to the barkeep for a rye 'Manhattan/Old Fashioned/Sazerac' (delete as appropriate). Repeat step 3 as needed.

Bar chat

○ Rye is notoriously difficult for distillers to work with. When the rye is ground and mixed with water it produces a particularly sticky, viscous mash.

○ Look out for classic examples of rye whiskey: Michter's Barrel Strength Straight Rye, Sazerac Straight Rye, Rittenhouse Straight Rye, Bulleit Rye, WhistlePig 10-year-old, Knob Creek Rye, George Dickel Rye, Hudson Manhattan Rye.

Teeling

Two brothers with Irish whiskey in their blood are leading the way for a new Irish whiskey revolution.

Pronunciation
As it looks.

What you need to know
- All of the whiskies from Teeling are very drinkable, with deep, rich flavours and gentle spice.
- In 2012, The Teeling Whiskey Company was founded as an independent bottler of Irish whiskey, founded by brothers Stephen and Jack Teeling. In 2015 they opened their own distillery, the first new distillery in Dublin for over 125 years.
- Their strong connection with the Irish whiskey industry meant that they could source a lot of ready-made and well-aged whiskey, so they could bottle top-quality, interesting whiskies straight off. Since their launch in 2012, Teeling have bottled a variety of award-winning whiskies, all sharing a rich, spicy and complex flavour, including single malt, blended and single grain whiskey.

Best enjoyed ...
Whilst hatching plans on the back of a beer mat, in a corner of a crowded panelled Dublin pub. The vision and change-maker attitude of the Teeling brothers is incredibly infectious, so you'll be inspired for your own venture.

Setting the scene

Weekend in Dublin! Take a trip with your pals and visit the new Teeling Whiskey Distillery, the Guinness Storehouse and the Old Jameson Distillery, which make up a boozy triangle all within walking distance of each other. It's virtually impossible to avoid having fun in Dublin so head to one of the old pubs in the evening and let yourself be swept away in the 'craic'. Just don't forget to pack the painkillers!

Bar chat

O The Teeling Brothers aren't just whisky makers, they are also reality TV stars. 'Whiskey Business', a three-part documentary, followed the journey of the Teeling brand and the building of their new distillery and was a big success in Ireland.

O Look out for Teeling single malt, a deliciously drinkable Irish whiskey. This whiskey has been finished in five types of wine cask. There are a lot of fruity and spicy notes, but also a soft strawberries-and-cream note as well.

Sullivans Cove

The most intrepid of whiskies on the Intrepid Line. Could this be the whisky that travels the furthest to get into your glass? A few years ago Tasmanian whisky was unthinkable, now it's a sensation!

What you need to know

- Whisky from Sullivans Cove is perfumed and floral, with lots of vanilla and spice.
- Like most distilleries, the choice of barrel is key to the Sullivans Cove flavour; they use bourbon and port casks to enhance the rich texture they get in the distillation process.
- However, they usually bottle their whiskies as single cask whisky, meaning that only one cask is bottled at a time rather than being blended with other whiskies. Because each cask is distinct, the whiskies are completely unique. They are very limited in number and highly sought-after.
- In 2014, when Sullivans Cove French Oak whisky won *Whisky Magazine*'s World Whisky Award, the demand for Sullivans Cove, and all other Tasmanian whiskies, took off literally overnight, and demand has not slipped in the slightest.

Best enjoyed ...

As a spot the difference. Whilst the 'New World' of whiskies share a lot of characteristics with single malt Scotch whisky there is a distinctive flavour, quite hard to pinpoint, that separates it from Scotch. As an excuse for a weeknight dram, schedule 'tasting practice' with a friend. Taste it side by side with a single malt Scotch whisky for an interesting comparison.

Setting the scene

Tasmania, or 'Tassie' as the Aussies call it, is relatively small in comparison to Australia – itis actually about the same size as Ireland. One of the best ways to get around is a 'self-drive' tour of the island as there are no passenger train services. Be sure to keep an eye on the road, as the stunning and dramatic scenery at every turn could be distracting. As well as the excellent Tasmanian Whisky Trail, make sure to factor in stops for the Tasmanian Beer Trail and Tasmanian Cider Trail.

Bar chat

O Tasmania has had a boom in whisky-making recently and has become a centre of excellence for whisky production. New distilleries are popping up all over the island. At the moment there are currently around eighteen distilleries on Tasmania, including Lark, Overeem, Nant and Hellyers Yard, worthy of a try.

O In the 1820s there were around fifteen distilleries (plus countless illicit stills) on Tasmania. In 1838 distilling was banned on the island of Tasmania. It was not until 1992, with the opening of Lark Distillery, that the 150-year dry spell was broken.

O Look out for Sullivans Cove American Oak cask: lots of lovely vanilla and citrussy fruit notes with a good deal of wood spice and nuts.

Glenlivet

Glenfiddich

Glenrothes

Arran

Balblair

Rum Wood Finish

Aberfeldy

Dalwhinnie

 Blend Wood finish T Type   Single malt

 Starting point

6. Amber Line

The Amber Line is the perfect line for people who have a sweet-tooth. These whiskies are easy-going, honeyed and fruity. They are also ideal for gifts, especially if you are buying for someone whose tastes you aren't sure of. It's hard not to like these nectarous whiskies. Their easy-drinking, simple nature means that they are not overly complex or challenging. Our journey will take us all around the Highlands and Speyside as well as taking in a hop over to the beautiful Isle of Arran.

When to take the Amber Line
If you are after something comforting and tasty you have come to the right line. These whiskies work extremely well as an après-dinner digestif with dessert. Although they would also be well-suited to 'avec-dinner', if you fancied having a dram with your scran.

Stations on the Amber Line
Glenfiddich, Glenlivet, Glenrothes, Arran, Balblair, Rum Wood Finish, Aberfeldy and Dalwhinnie.

Glenfiddich

See the Heart Line p. 33.

Glenlivet

See the Heart Line p. 35.

Glenrothes

Glenrothes is the joining point from Glenfiddich and Glenlivet on the Amber Line and a wonderfully rich whisky. Located in the bustling Speyside town of Rothes, not to be confused with the post-World War II-designed town of the same name in Fife.

Pronunciation
Glen-Roth-Iss

What you need to know
- A soft but complex dram offering up lots of vanilla and fresh, fruit salad flavours.
- Glenrothes bottlings are known as vintages. Unlike other distilleries that combine whiskies of the same age or older to produce 10 years, 12 years, 15 years etc, Glenrothes is bottled when they feel it has matured sufficiently. The year it was distilled and put into cask appears on the label, e.g. 2001 Vintage (see How whisky is made, p. 14). These vintages are released when they are considered ready and the bottling date is noted on the label (which allows you to calculate the age); the actual age at which a whisky is bottled might differ from year to year.

○ Within this process Glenrothes uses a number of previously used bourbon and sherry casks, this means the flavour released from the cask is more subtle and three-dimensional.

Best enjoyed ...
Over a good natter with a friend. Glenrothes has enough complexity to keep your palate entertained but not distracted from the conversation at hand. It works equally well as a digestif or aperitif or with any course of your meal.

Setting the scene
Take a trip down the River Spey in a canoe to really experience the river that this whole region is named after. Dry off in the Mash Tun in Aberlour, a real gem of a pub. Speyside is a beautiful wilderness that can only really be appreciated by getting out into it. Traditionally people would have experienced the stunning landscapes whilst hunting, shooting and fishing, but these days you can explore it more ethically on foot or mountain bike.

Bar chat
○ The shape of the Glenrothes bottle is quite distinctive and is inspired by the rounded shape of traditional whisky sample bottles used by master blenders.
○ Look out for Glenrothes Vintage 2001, a tasty tipple of creamy vanilla and cherry tart with lots of soft spiced cinnamon and freshly cut apples.

Arran

A relative newcomer in the whisky industry, Arran Distillery, at Lochranza on the north coast of the Isle of Arran, first ran its stills in 1995 and has now gained a loyal following of whisky enthusiasts across the globe who eagerly await each new limited release.

Pronunciation

A-ran

What you need to know

- Arran whiskies are known for being jam-packed full of sweet, fruity flavour. Think apples, pears, syrup and sweet vanilla spices of cinnamon and nutmeg.
- The Arran Distillery is the first on the Isle of Arran since 1837, when the distillery at Lagg closed. Like many of the Hebridean islands, Arran has a unique micro-climate warmed by the Gulf Stream, which could influence the maturation process and so increase the sweet flavours from the casks.
- Arran whiskies are popular amongst enthusiasts because they tend to bottle at higher alcohol levels, which most people see as a bonus. They also avoid chill-filtering and adding caramel to maintain the natural character of the whisky.

Best enjoyed ...

In the bath. Draw a warm bath and complete the Arran experience with some Arran Aromatics soaps, made at Brodick on the island. Let the aromas from the bubble bath ease your mind as you soak in the tub warming from the inside out and the outside in.

Setting the scene

Arran is a stunning island to visit, particularly in the summer months (it can be a bit bleak in the winter). For the outdoorsy type there is plenty to do, from mountain biking to hiking and kayaking. Arran has become something of a foodie paradise, with locally produced cheeses, ice creams, oatcakes and more, so there's plenty to explore for the more sedentary too. Like many of the Scottish islands, which look so close to the mainland, it takes a surprisingly long time to get there. You can take the summer ferry from the Kintyre peninsula which is about three hours' drive from Glasgow. It is worth it.

Bar chat

- The Arran Distillery won't be alone on the island for much longer. A new distillery is being built at the site of the old distillery at Lagg, where they will be making a peated whisky too.
- Look out for Arran 18-year-old, the oldest Arran expression in the core range, a delicious fruity, creamy dram bottled at 46 per cent abv which has a long, lingering finish. A peated single malt from Arran Distillery known as Machrie Moor is also very popular.

Balblair

A classic Highland-style malt whisky. With lots of fruit cake, woody spice and warming dried fruits and nut flavours.

Pronunciation
Bal-Blair

What you need to know

○ Whisky from Balblair is distinctly fruity and spicy with a robust, leathery note to it.

○ Like Glenrothes, Balblair opt for vintages instead of age statements on their labels, so instead of being a 10-year-old, a whisky might be a 2006 vintage. Each whisky will age slightly differently because of the weather and seasonal conditions, which means whiskies are released when they are ready, so they may be different ages when released and out of chronological order.

○ Balblair Distillery is the location for the dramatic final scenes of the fantastic film *The Angels' Share*, which has become a cult classic, with whisky in the lead role.

Best enjoyed ...

Celebrating your own vintage! As one of the few whiskies with an actual year on, it's a real treat to try your own vintage. That whisky has been maturing for exactly the same amount of time as you! A word of advice: the longer you live, the harder and more expensive it will be for you to find whiskies of your birth year, so if you are keen to get your own or someone else's birth year vintage, buy them when you spot the vintage for sale and save them for a 'special' birthday.

Setting the scene

Balblair is another of the distilleries you can visit if you are travelling the North Coast 500 road. Most people see whisky as quite a contemplative drink, and you can see why when you visit the remote distilleries like Balblair. You really get a sense of the Highlands there: big sky, fresh air, space and freedom. Breathe it in!

○ Balblair is thought to be one of the oldest distilleries in Scotland, dating back to 1790, although there was probably illicit distilling going on at the same location for some time before this.

○ Look out for the Balblair 2005 vintage. A woody, vanilla dram, with hints of spice and syrup along with some more delicate, floral notes.

Rum Wood Finish

A relatively rarely seen type of wood finish. Whiskies that have been partially matured in rum casks have, as you would imagine, delicious and interesting tropical fruit notes that instantly transport you to the Caribbean.

What you need to know

○ Rum-finished whiskies create a tropical melange in your mouth. Rum is traditionally made with molasses, so the casks carry an intensely sweet note and all the tropical flavours of the Caribbean. Think pineapples, melons, mangos, papayas, passion-fruit and coconut notes.

○ Ex-rum casks, of good quality, are notoriously difficult for distilleries to source, mainly because the casks that rum distilleries use to mature their rum can often be completely exhausted, they are so old and have been used so many times they are literally falling apart.

○ Some whisky distilleries have found a way to work around this problem though: they fill ex-bourbon barrels with their own blend of rums and leave the rum to soak into the casks. Then when it's 'ready' they drain the rum out, and put in the whisky for 'finishing'.

Best enjoyed …

With coconut water on the beach of a tropical island. Served long with lots of ice, a ratio of 1 part whisky to 2 parts coconut water is ideal. That's tropical paradise in a glass!

Setting the scene

Do you need an excuse to visit the home of rum and hit the Caribbean Islands? Didn't think so! Rum-finished whiskies adopt the spirit of the Caribbean and are less 'pretentious' than other whiskies; you should channel the 'don't worry, be happy vibe' when you are drinking them. Rum is thought to have originated in Barbados, so start your tour there and indulge in one of the other local specialities… rum-infused hot sauce!

Bar chat

○ Look out for these classic examples: Balvenie Caribbean Cask 14-year-old, Glenfiddich Gran Reserva 21-year-old or Benriach Dark Rum Finish 15-year-old. All exquisite examples of Rum Wood Finished whiskies.

Aberfeldy

From the geographical 'heart of Scotland', Aberfeldy, in Perthshire. Aberfeldy whisky tastes just like a classic Highland malt should.

Pronunciation
A-Burr-Fell-Dee

What you need to know

○ Aberfeldy has lots of honey, toffee, fudge notes as well as hints of spice and heather.

- The water source for Aberfeldy Distillery is the Pitilie Burn, famed for having deposits of alluvial gold. For this reason Aberfeldy is sometimes known as 'the golden dram'.
- The distillery was founded by John Dewar of Dewar's whisky fame, a true entrepreneur and one of the early whisky barons who helped make Scotch whisky what it is today (see Dewar's on the Heart Line, p. 25).

Best enjoyed ...

With fine dark chocolate. First take a bite of chocolate and let it melt on your tongue, then take a sip of whisky. Now reverse the process: take a sip of whisky, and before swallowing it take a nibble of chocolate. The alcohol from the whisky will mix with the melting chocolate as it warms on your tongue, quite delicious!

Setting the scene

Aberfeldy is a great place to base yourself for a tour of central Scotland. To the north, the wilds of Aviemore for climbing, and skiing in the winter; to the east, Dundee for a trip to the brand new V&A Museum; to the south-west, Loch Lomond. And lots of scenery in between! If you need some chocolate inspiration to try with your whisky, you could do worse than a visit to Iain Burnett Highland Chocolatier, which is only ten minutes' drive away from the distillery. You may already be familiar with them if you frequently fly first class on British Airways; if not, you are in for a treat!

Bar chat

- You can't miss 'The Puggy Engine', a wee train engine that used to take barley and casks to the distillery, and then take the whisky to market. These days it's a bit of a tourist attraction, however it was once vital to the local area and distillery, which were reliant on the rail connections. In 1966, during the national modernisation of the British rail

network, the line was closed permanently, which had a major impact on the local area and the distillery.
- ○ Look out for Aberfeldy 12-year-old: warming and smooth, this honeyed and malty whisky also has light floral notes to it.

Dalwhinnie

Perhaps one of the most scenic locations for a distillery in the Highlands. As you drive up the A9 towards Aviemore keep an eye out on the left-hand side, you can't miss it.

Pronunciation
Dal-Whinn-Ee

What you need to know
- ○ Dalwhinnie is a clean, crisp-tasting Highland whisky. It has lots of heather honey tones and malty, nutty notes.
- ○ Dalwhinnie is one of only a few distilleries that use worm tubs (see Glossary, p. 139) to condense the spirit vapour back into liquid. This happens more slowly than the conventional method and gives the whisky a heavier and more robust texture.
- ○ If you're planning to visit, make sure you are dressed suitably: this is one of highest distilleries you can visit in the UK at just under 2000 feet, and one of the coldest inhabited places in the UK with a year-round average temperature of 6.6 °C. It also has one of the lowest average annual hours of sunshine in the UK.

Best enjoyed ...

On a very snowy day, the kind of horizontal, blustery snow the Scots are well-acquainted with. Get inside somewhere and thaw yourself by the fire with a dram of Dalwhinnie.

Setting the scene

Clear days are very rare at Dalwhinnie, due to its geographic location and altitude. For this reason Dalwhinnie practically experiences a subpolar oceanic climate, like much of Iceland. This being said, it is definitely worth braving the elements and visiting the beautifully picturesque distillery.

Bar chat

- The distillery also acts as a weather station. The distillery manager has to take daily weather and temperature readings for the Met Office.
- In the 1980s the distillery decided to remove the worm tubs (see Glossary, p. 139) and fit shell and tube condensers instead. The character of the new make spirit changed so much that the worm tubs had to be refitted.
- Look out for Dalwhinnie 15-year-old, a mainstay of the Classic Malts range.

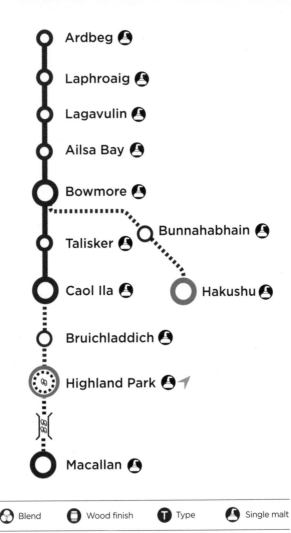

Ardbeg

Laphroaig

Lagavulin

Ailsa Bay

Bowmore

Talisker

Bunnahabhain

Caol Ila

Hakushu

Bruichladdich

Highland Park

Macallan

 Blend

Wood finish

 Type

 Single malt

Starting point

 Foot path

Ferry line

7. Outliers Line

The Outlier island is a representation of the traditional island whiskies of Scotland and not a specific, geographic island, although many come from the home of the island whisky, Islay (pronounced Aye-la). These whiskies are called the Outliers for a reason: they have extreme flavours and are often made by people pushing the boundaries in terms of both flavour and the elements, which is why, on the WhiskyTubeMap, you need to get a boat to the island, crossing the flavour threshold. The ferries represent the gateway to a new whisky palate and the stations positioned between the mainland and the island are good ones to try as a starting point. Expect to experience some or all of the following tastes and aromas in varying degrees of intensity: peat smoke, soot, charcoal, ash, cigars, tobacco, log fires, coal, medicine cabinets, carbolic soap, TCP, fishiness, seaweed, salt, brine and so on. You have been warned. But don't let these flavours put you off, these whiskies are wonderfully crafted and can open your eyes to how enjoyable smoky whiskies can be.

When to take the Outliers Line
Don't dive right into the Outliers Line, there have been many instances of people having a smoky whisky as their first-ever whisky and it putting them off for the rest of their lives. It's a preference thing, but it needs building up to.

Try Outlier whiskies with a cheese board. They work

particularly well with strong blue cheeses, like Roquefort, Stilton or Gorgonzola as well as hard cheeses like Pecorino Romano or Parmesan.

Stations on the Outliers Line
Bunnahabhain, Bruichladdich, Caol Ila, Talisker, Bowmore, Ailsa Bay, Lagavulin, Laphroaig and Ardbeg.

Bunnahabhain

Stop off at Bunnahabhain en route to the Outlier island to prepare your palate for the island flavours of peat and smoke. This is a whisky that allows you to dip your toe into that world.

Pronunciation
Boo-Nah-Hav-Enn

What you need to know
- With Bunnahbhain, you experience a faint hint of smoke which is balanced by soft fruits and nuts with a lovely malty-sweet finish.
- A surprisingly light and fresh-tasting whisky, considering it comes from Islay, which is famed for its fiery, smoky and pungent drams. Bunnahabhain uses a very lightly peated malted barley compared to other Islay malts.
- Bunnahabhain is one of a select number of distilleries who have taken the decision to stop using artificial colour and chill-filtering and to bottle at a higher strength. So you get unadulterated whisky straight from the cask.

Best enjoyed ...

At sea! Boat is the best way to see the Scottish islands and a bottle of Bunnahabhain is the perfect 'grog' to have with you. With its slight maritime influence and earthy flavours it will warm your cockles and remind you of dry land, particularly useful if you are struggling to find your sea-legs.

Setting the scene

Bunnahabhain can be found on the Isle of Islay, which, in the right weather can be explored on foot or by bike. Adapt your watch to 'Islay time' and take in the breathtaking scenery, look out for wildlife and gaze out over the Sound of Islay to Jura, all from the winding single-track road from Port Askaig to Bunnahabhain. If you are in the car and have to pull into a passing place to let a vehicle by, don't forget the obligatory 'Islay wave' (a raise of the hand or a finger to acknowledge the other driver). With so few cars on the island everyone tends to acknowledge everyone else; it will leave you feeling like an 'Ileach' in no time.

Bar chat

O Look out for Bunnahabhain 12-year-old, a light and fresh whisky with hints of seaweed, leather and sweet dark cherries, with a faint whisper of smoke.

Bruichladdich

The famously maverick and disruptive Bruichladdich are self-styled 'progressive Hebridean distillers'. They are immensely proud of their traditional and authentic approach to distilling with a strong emphasis put on 'terroir', because they believe that the specific environment, conditions and climate impart unique flavour characteristics in the final product.

Pronunciation:
Broo-Ic-Laddie

What you need to know

O Bruichladdich's core range of whiskies is unpeated, breaking from the norm of the other famous malt whiskies on the island. Bruichladdich's whiskies are exceptionally fruity, with lots of pear drop and green apple flavours, followed by some peppery spice and a reminder of sweet sugar puffs. The finish is fresh, crisp and long lasting.

O Unlike many other distilleries, they mature all of their whisky on the island, as they believe that the terroir of the island plays an important role in the maturation of their whiskies.

O They are pioneers in experimenting with cask finishing or 'ACEing' (Additional Cask Evolution) in Bruichladdich's parlance. Which means that you will find some weird and wonderful cask finishes and one-offs in their range.

Best enjoyed ...
Bruichladdich is a great whisky for a gathering – the kind of gathering that happens a lot in pubs around the islands and Highlands of Scotland, or that you can recreate in your living room. You need plenty of people, some musical instruments, some furniture to push back for a dancefloor and a general sense of fun and cosy. Oh, and a bottle of Bruichladdich to pass around.

Setting the scene

The spirit of Bruichladdich is no greater than during Feis Ile (The Islay Festival of Music and Malt) held at the end of May every year. It's not the quietest time to visit, but the party atmosphere brings the island to life in a very special way. No visit to Islay would be complete without a tour at Bruichladdich, which during the festival sees some 3000 people pass through its gates to celebrate its annual open day. Make sure to book a tour, as the cult following of Bruichladdich makes it high on the list of whisky fanatics visiting the island.

Bar chat

O Bruichladdich's motto is 'Clachan a Choin', in Scottish Gaelic; this literally translates as 'the dog's bollocks'!

O The distillery produces three types of spirit: Bruichladdich (unpeated), Port Charlotte (heavily peated) and Octomore (super heavily peated), and all share the tradition-meets-experimentation style.

O Look out for Bruichladdich Scottish Barley: The Laddie Classic, a wonderfully sweet and fruity whisky from Bruichladdich. Think Werther's Originals with freshly sliced Red Delicious apples followed by more toffee and honey notes.

Caol Ila

Of all the classic peaty Islay malts, Caol Ila is perhaps one of the more easy-drinking. It makes an excellent entry point for someone looking to get to grips with peated whisky.

Pronunciation

Cull-Eela

What you need to know

○ Whisky from Caol Ila has a salty sea air-ness to it as well as a good amount of smoke, which makes it feisty, but not so much it will blow your head off.

○ Caol Ila is a really under-appreciated Islay whisky compared to its more famous island neighbours. Of the eight distilleries on Islay, it is the largest but not the best-known, giving it an under-the-radar cachet.

○ The stillroom (the part of the distillery where the copper pot stills are) at Caol Ila boasts, by far and away, one of the most spectacular views of any stillroom in Scotland.

Best enjoyed ...

As an aperitif, on the rocks while eating gigantic, black, briney olives. The ice will help lock down some of the smoke, and the saltiness of the olives will help accentuate the flavours in your mouth.

Setting the scene

Caol Ila is not only a treat for your palate, it's one for your eyes too. It's probably the easiest distillery to get to from the main landing spot of Port Askaig, so if you've not got long on Islay head straight there, and prepare yourself for the view from the stillroom, right across the Sound of Islay.

Bar chat

○ About once a year Caol Ila produces a small batch of unpeated whisky for an annual special release. These are worth looking out for as they allow you to have an interesting insight into the differences between the peated and unpeated whisky from Caol Ila.

○ Look out for Caol Ila 12-year-old, a deliciously smooth-tasting Islay malt whisky. This dram is wonderful to try if you've never experienced peated whisky before. The peat is delicately balanced, with soft fruits and a salty oiliness.

Talisker

Not all Outliers come from Islay. Talisker is a robust and rugged whisky, not dissimilar to the landscape on its home, the island of Skye.

Pronunciation
Tal-Iss-Kur

What you need to know

- Whisky from Talisker has a double nature, it has a base of smooth, calming, fruity aromas and flavours that suddenly leap into pinnacles of smoke and peat.

- The Isle of Skye is rugged and wild and Talisker reflects this; many consider it to have maritime qualities, a bit like the ones you find in whiskies on the Coastal Line (p. 51), along with the more island style of smoke and peat.

- Despite the distillery burning to the ground in 1960, it was rebuilt with identical stills in order to maintain consistency of flavour as closely as possible. They use a double distillation process to give the whisky a rich, smooth base for all those rugged flavours.

- Talisker is the only distillery on the island of Skye, although a legend dating back to Bonnie Prince Charlie has it that Drambuie, a whisky-based liqueur, originated on the island.

Best enjoyed ...

Head for the hills and take a hip flask of Talisker. It's a great whisky to have on a walk with you, particularly if you're in need of some inspiration. The tranquillity, beauty and sheer brute force of the island will help you indulge your imagination.

Setting the scene

Skye is a magical place, the landscape of the entire island is completely unspoiled and incredibly dramatic – you may think you have ended up in Middle Earth. You can get there by ferry from Mallaig, which you can reach by taking the Harry Potter train (the 'Jacobite Steam Train') from Fort William. The Cuillins, a rocky mountain range whose highest peak in the Black Cuillins is 992 metres, dominate the skyline, and the glens provide tranquil contrast. Being on the island doesn't mean slumming it; there are a number of Michelin-starred restaurants like Kinloch Lodge or the Three Chimneys, where the seafood is particularly good.

Bar chat

O A new distillery on Skye is currently under construction on the southern peninsula of Sleat at Torabhaig.

O Look out for Talisker 57° North, and bottled at 57 per cent abv; the name represents the location of the distillery at a latitude of 57 degrees north. This is a dramatic whisky, full of undulating twists and turns for smoke as well as peppery spices and limey citrus notes.

Bowmore

Bowmore is a great way on and off the Outlier island, linking the softer flavours of the top of the WhiskyTubeMap with the peaty, smoky flavours of the island.

Pronunciation

Bow-More

What you need to know

O A sweet and softly smoky whisky. A brilliant dram to explore if you are ready to take your next steps into the world of peat and Islay malts.

O Bowmore is the oldest distillery on Islay, founded in 1779. It lies in the heart of the town of Bowmore, the administrative capital of Islay and is one of the top-selling whiskies from Islay.

O It is also one of only a few distilleries that still use a traditional floor malting to malt a proportion of their barley, the rest of which they will try to source from Islay, although some may also come from the mainland. The traditional process of floor malting is kept to preserve the tradition, something that is incredibly important for the whisky heritage, even if it does cost more!

Best enjoyed ...

Bowmore has a number of different expressions or styles within their range; why not try them (almost) side by side on a mini pub crawl of Bowmore? Or recreate your own at home with some friends and a few bottles.

Setting the scene

If you aren't too keen on boats you could always fly to Islay from Glasgow airport. The flight may not be for the faint-hearted, but you'll be out of the airport and at the distillery within minutes – there can't be many other places you can say that! It's so easy to go distillery-hopping when you are on Islay you will need to book hold luggage, otherwise you won't be able to bring your purchases back.

Bar chat

O The MacTaggart Leisure Centre and swimming pool, housed in a former warehouse adjacent to Bowmore Distillery, uses surplus heat from the production process to heat the

- swimming pool, a very innovative and energy-efficient idea.
- Look out for Bowmore Darkest 15-year-old: this whisky spends its final three years in Oloroso sherry butts, which give it a delicious dark fruit note. The raisins and sweetness of the sherry expertly mask some of the smoke in this whisky, the sweetness then prevails in the finish, quite delicious!

Ailsa Bay

Ailsa Bay is definitely an Outlier. Although it takes its name from an island it is actually a mainlaind whisky that has adopted some island flavours.

Pronunciation
Ale-Sa Bay

What you need to know
- Ailsa Bay's whisky is described as having the perfect balance of sweet and peat. It is lovely and cinnamony, with muesli cereal notes and a drying peat smoke.
- Ailsa Bay is an excellent example of a single malt that doesn't comply with the idea that 'traditional' geographical regions equals a certain style of whisky. Ailsa Bay is a Lowland whisky that is quite heavily peated whereas, traditionally speaking, Lowland whiskies are light, fruity and fresh-tasting.
- Ailsa Bay undergoes an interesting 'micro-maturation', where the new make spirit is first put into very small Hudson Baby Bourbon casks, between 25 litres and 100 litres, to kick-start the maturation, before being transferred to a mix of standard-sized ex-bourbon and virgin oak casks.

Best enjoyed ...

When you can't decide if you want a peaty whisky or a sweet whisky. With Ailsa Bay you will get the best of both.

Setting the scene

The uninhabited island of Ailsa Craig lies 10 miles off the south-west coast from Girvan on the Scottish mainland. Ailsa Bay takes its name from this island, which is famous for providing the granite that makes curling stones. The island, which is approximately two miles in circumference, was recently on the market for £1.5m (originally listed as £2.5m). It would make an ideal location for a wannabe Bond Villain's lair, already replete with helipad and jetty.

Bar chat

O Built in just six months in 2007 within the grounds of the William Grant & Sons Girvan Grain Distillery, this distillery was created to provide a variety of different single malts to give them more options for their blended whisky, Grants.

O Look out for the eponymously named Ailsa Bay, the inaugural release from the distillery. The whisky is sweet, like liquorice, but balanced with smoky hints of tar and soot. There is a small piece of Ailsa Craig granite in the stopper of each bottle.

Lagavulin

Nestled between the equally esteemed distilleries of Laphroaig to the west and Ardbeg to the east, Lagavulin is distinctively different from its neighbours, which is good if you find other Outliers a bit peaty.

Pronunciation
La-Ga-Vool-In

What you need to know
O Despite being a heavily peated Islay whisky, Lagavulin is refined and has balanced flavours of sweet dried fruits and spice; it isn't just all peat and nothing else. It is slightly less medicinal/iodine-y than its Kildalton neighbours due to the additional sweetness found in Lagavulin.

O Lagavulin is well known for doing things very slowly; it has a long fermentation and a very long distillation, supposedly the slowest on Islay, allowing for the maximum amount of reflux, which creates a very soft and well-rounded spirit.

O Lagavulin is a real connoisseurs' Islay whisky: the flavours are well refined, there is plenty of peat and smoke but it isn't overwhelming and doesn't mask the other sweeter and fruity aromas in the whisky.

Best enjoyed...
While reading a Scottish crime novel. If you are after a whisky-fuelled novel then *Smokeheads* by Doug Johnstone is ideal. A fantastic tale of four whisky-loving friends who go to Islay for a lads' weekend, where everything that could possibly go wrong does go wrong.

Setting the scene

Why not charter a yacht and head to Lagavulin by sea, which would be a wonderful way to experience all of Islay's eight distilleries. Many of them have their own private jetties. Hire a crew to take care of the hard work so you can kick back and enjoy the drams as you tour around the island in style.

Bar chat

○ Malt Mill Distillery operated on the same site as Lagavulin until 1962. A special, albeit fictitious, cask of Malt Mill was a key part of the plot of the movie *The Angels' Share*.

○ Look out for Lagavulin 16-year-old, a real classic Islay single malt, sweet dried fruits and a drying smoky peat intertwined with an unexpected smoothness. No wonder this has become such a highly revered staple amongst whisky enthusiasts.

Laphroaig

A real 'marmite' whisky: you'll love it or you'll hate it!

Pronunciation

La-froyg

What you need to know

○ Whisky from Laphroaig will give you a wallop of smoke on the first sip, you'll then get a good punch of seaweed and full-on medicinal notes, which then soften to a delicate sweetness. Don't let this put you off, it all combines to something that is pleasantly surprising.

○ During prohibition Laphroaig was the only whisky legally imported into the USA. The notably strong smell of 'iodine' from the whisky led customs officials to believe that it had

medicinal properties. The iodine smell is classic to peaty whiskies, and many come to love it.

O The extra peatiness is a decision made by Laphroaig, who dry their malted barley with peat for over 12 hours to give it an exceptionally peaty flavour. The longer the barley is dried with peat, the peatier the whisky will be.

O You can claim your own square foot of Islay by purchasing a bottle of Laphroaig. If you visit the distillery you can collect your 'rent' (a miniature whisky) and visit your square foot – wellies are provided!

Best enjoyed ...

After a long walk in a rainstorm. Sip by a roaring wood fire as you dry off. The warmth of the whisky will have you feeling toasty in no time!

Setting the scene

Head to the south-east coast of Islay, watching out for peat bogs. Take the newly completed South Distilleries Path to walk or cycle from Laphroaig to Lagavulin and Ardbeg. A short distance beyond Ardbeg in the old churchyard of Kildalton Parish Church stands the Kildalton Cross, a beautifully carved monolithic Celtic cross from 800 AD.

Bar chat

O In 1994 the distillery was issued Prince Charles' Royal Warrant. It is said that Prince Charles was particularly fond of Laphroaig 15-year-old, a now discontinued expression.

O Look out for the wonderfully rich Laphroaig Quarter Cask. This whisky is matured for a short time in very small quarter casks. This gives the whisky more contact with the wood, and the result is spectacular. A woody, smoky, yet surprisingly tropical whisky!

Ardbeg

The end of the Outlier Line, with just cause as Ardbeg whiskies are a bit like biting into a piece of charcoaled driftwood that has been saturated with seawater, but in a really good kind of way!

Pronunciation
Ard-Beg

What you need to know
- Ardbeg is famed for producing one of the peatiest whiskies on Islay. Prepare your palate for a punch of peat, followed by smoked fish and bacon with seawater notes, menthol Fisherman's Friends and a delicate sweet citrus note. Complex, smoky and powerful, simply amazing.
- It has a very loyal following of hardcore peat-loving fans. So it is almost unthinkable to know that Ardbeg was closed down completely in 1983 and not reopened until 1989, at which point it was considered too peaty! Amazing what a bit of imagination and TLC has created.
- The three Kildalton distilleries (the others being Laphroaig and Lagavulin) share a lot of DNA: same location, same raw ingredients, same peaty characteristic, etc., yet the three whiskies are undeniably different, an example of the 'magic of whisky' that happens every time a whisky is left in the cask.

Best enjoyed ...
In the wee sma' hours (read: after midnight). A wonderful late-night session dram. You don't want to start on Ardbeg too early in an evening or you won't be able to taste anything else because of all the peat.

Setting the scene

If you are a fitness enthusiast as well as a whisky enthusiast, you may well enjoy entering the famous Ardbeg Half-Marathon. Held annually since 1986, on a good day it could be one of the most scenic half-marathon locations in the UK; however, on a bad day you could be running head first into gale force winds for 7 miles of the 13-mile route. No prize for guessing what the winners' prizes are.

Bar chat

- In 2011, Ardbeg sent samples of their whisky to the International Space Station, as part of an experiment on how gravity (or lack thereof) affects maturation: cosmic whisky!
- If you want more peated whisky in your life, then you should join the Ardbeg Committee to get access to special 'Committee Only' exclusives.
- Look out for Ardbeg Uigadal (Oog-Ah-Dal): named after the loch that provides the distillery's water source, this whisky is a marriage of bourbon and sherry-matured Ardbeg. The smoke isn't overpowering and the sweet honeyed fruit cake and maltiness balances very well indeed. This is a real favourite.

Food

Robert Burns famously wrote 'Freedom an' whisky gang thegither!' (freedom and whisky go together) but what you may not know is that whisky and food also go together brilliantly.

Whisky and food pairings are becoming increasingly popular. Until you try it, you may not realise the difference that happens in your mouth when enjoying whisky with food, as compared to drinking whisky simply on its own. By pairing whisky with something to eat you are not just enhancing your whisky experience, you are actually looking for ways in which the food will help you discover more about the whisky and how whisky can help you get even more flavour from the food.

Try taking nibbles of food and sips of neat or slightly watered whisky, alternating between which you do first, and let the flavours mix on your tongue.

A few pointers to get you going in the right direction:

O Don't always think of the obvious pairings, where you match the flavour of a whisky to the flavour of the food, like a smoked fish and a smoky whisky, these tend to be too overpowering. Look for complementing flavours. A whisky that tastes of oranges would go better with something like duck or chicken than with a dish containing orange.
  O E.g. a smoked salmon would work well with a lighter, fresh, citrussy whisky to contrast with the strong smoky fish (think Easy Loop, p. 41).

- O Think about the richness of the dish and pair whisky accordingly, as with wine, where a light wine will go well with a light-tasting meal.
- O Fatty and oily foods work particularly well with medium-rich whiskies and help accentuate the fatty flavours in the food and mouthfeel of the whisky.
    - O E.g. a classic roast beef with Yorkshire puddings and rich gravy would work very well with sherried and fruity whiskies (think Decadent Line (p. 63) or Heart Line (p. 21)).
- O Spicy foods such as Indian and Mexican can work with whiskies too, just make sure the whisky isn't too spicy or peppery. Note that any sort of chilli spice will be accentuated by the alcohol in the whisky.
    - O E.g. a spicy lamb jalfrezi curry with a balanced sweet and fruity whisky (think Heart Line (p. 21)).

Here are a few examples of classic flavour pairings between food and styles of whisky using the WhiskyTubeMap lines:

Chocolate
Dark chocolate (70 per cent cocoa solids or more) works well with:
- O Amber Line (p. 91)
- O Decadent Line (p. 63)

Milk chocolate works well with:
- O Easy Loop (p. 41)
- O Heart Line (p. 21)

Cheese
Soft and creamy cheese (like blue cheese or Camembert/Brie) works well with:
- O Outliers Line (p. 103)
- O Coastal Line (p. 51)

Hard or smoked cheeses work well with:

O Heart Line (p. 21)
O Amber Line (p. 91)

Popcorn

Sweet popcorn works well with:

O Intrepid Line (p. 79)
O Easy Loop (p. 41)

Salty/savoury popcorn works well with:

O Coastal Line (p. 51)
O Decadent Line (p. 63)

Ice cream

The combination of cold ice cream or sorbet and warming whiskies creates a real taste sensation.

Sorbets work well with:

O Easy Loop (p. 41)
O Amber Line (p. 91)

Vanilla ice cream works well with:

O Heart Line (p. 21)
O Amber Line (p. 91)

Chocolate ice cream works well with:

O Decadent Line (p. 63)

Cocktails

Don't forget, there are no rules when it comes to whisky. Whisky cocktails are an excellent way of experiencing, and even enhancing, the style and flavours of a whisky.

All of these cocktails are easy to make at home. And the 'bar tools' are easily replaced with kitchen implements:

O Use an empty jam-jar instead of a cocktail shaker.
O Use the end of a rolling pin instead of a muddler.
O Crush ice using a rolling pin to smash the ice in a sandwich bag.

The cocktails start out very straightforward and require a bit more measuring of ingredients as the list progresses.

Once you've tried making these cocktails once or twice you'll get the hang of them and in no time you'll be ready to host your own whisky-cocktail cocktail-party. *Madmen* eat your heart out!

Whisky and Soda/Highball

A great way to drink whisky on a hot day, if you're feeling thirsty or if you find whisky flavours a bit overpowering. See Hibiki on p. 29 for more details.

Line recommendation: Easy Loop

O 50 ml whisky
O Soda water

Pour whisky over ice in a long glass. Top with soda water. Stir and serve.

Whisky and ginger ale/Mamie Taylor

A very under-appreciated whisky serve. Crisp and refreshing, a great alternative to a G&T. Try with ginger beer if you want more ginger spice.

Line recommendation: Easy Loop

- O 50 ml whisky
- O Ginger ale

Pour whisky over ice in a long glass. Top up with ginger ale. Stir and serve.

Smoky Cokey

This is a great way to get into peaty and smoky whiskies – some might think this is sacrilegious. Trust us – it works!

Line recommendation: Outlier Line

- O 50 ml whisky
- O Cola (try cherry cola)

Pour whisky over ice in a long glass. Top up with (cherry) cola. Stir and serve.

Whisky and Coconut Water

Feeling tropical or wish the weather were better? This is guaranteed to bring the sunshine!

Line recommendation: Amber Line

- O 50 ml whisky
- O Coconut water

Pour whisky over ice in a long glass. Top up with coconut water. Stir and serve.

Boiler Maker/Hauf 'n' hauf

Not strictly speaking a cocktail. Drink whisky 'pub style' with a beer. Alternate between sips of beer and whisky.

Line recommendation: Heart Line

- O Pint of beer
- O Shot of whisky

Mizuwari

A ritual in the whisky bars of Tokyo, the Mizuwari is the classic Japanese whisky cocktail. See Yamazaki on p. 69 for more details.

Line recommendation: Decadent Line

- O 50 ml whisky (1 part)
- O Still mineral water (2 parts)

Pour whisky over ice in a long glass. Stir thirteen and a half times. Add more ice. Add two parts still mineral water. Stir three and a half times. Serve.

Old Fashioned

Possibly the most classic of all whisky cocktails. Watch out when ordering in a bar, the stirring takes a while!

Line recommendation: Coastal Line

- O 50 ml whisky
- O 2 dashes Angostura Bitters
- O Sugar cube

Pour two dashes of Angostura Bitters over a sugar cube in the bottom of an Old Fashioned glass or tumbler. Muddle the sugar cube to dissolve the sugar. Pour the whisky over and top up with ice. Stir for several minutes. The ice will melt into the cocktail as you stir, this dilutes it to a good length for sipping. As the ice melts add more ice cubes into the glass. Serve once stirring and ice dilution is sufficient.

Manhattan/Rob Roy

Another absolute classic, great for cocktail parties and aperitifs.

Line recommendation: Heart Line
- 50 ml whisky
- 25 ml sweet vermouth
- Dash Angostura Bitters

Add all ingredients to a stirring glass. Fill with ice. Stir for about a minute. Strain and pour into a chilled martini glass. Garnish with a cocktail cherry. Serve.

Sazerac

The official cocktail of New Orleans. Bring the Mardi Gras festivities to your home by serving these at a party.

Line recommendation: Intrepid Line
- 50 ml whisky
- 10 ml absinthe
- 3 dashes of Peychaud's Bitters
- Sugar cube

Pour three dashes of Peychaud's Bitters over a sugar cube in the bottom of an Old Fashioned glass or tumbler. Muddle sugar cube to dissolve the sugar. Add 50 ml whisky. In a separate, pre-chilled Old Fashioned glass, coat the inside of the glass with absinthe. Drain off excess absinthe. Pour the whisky mixture into the absinthe-rinsed glass. Garnish with twist of lemon peel. Serve.

Blood and Sand

Named after a bullfighter movie from 1922, this classic cocktail is equally tart and sweet.

Line recommendation: Decadent Line
- 25 ml whisky
- 25 ml sweet vermouth

- O 25 ml Cherry Heering
- O 25 ml (blood) orange juice

Add all ingredients to a cocktail shaker. Add ice and shake hard. Strain into a chilled martini glass. Garnish with a cherry. Serve.

Mint Julep

The official drink of the Kentucky Derby. See Kentucky Straight Bourbon on p. 32 for more details.

Line recommendation: Heart Line
- O 50 ml whisky
- O Sugar cube
- O Fresh mint (8 leaves approx.)

Muddle mint with sugar cube and a splash of water in the bottom of an Old Fashioned glass (or classic pewter Julep cup if you want to be authentic). Once the sugar dissolves, add 50 ml whisky. Top up with crushed ice. Stir until glass starts to frost on outside. Garnish with sprig of mint. Serve.

Whisky Sour

Another classic cocktail. With or without egg whites this is a zingy-tasting cocktail.

Line recommendation: Outliers Line
- O 50 ml whisky
- O 25 ml lemon juice
- O 2 tsp sugar syrup
- O 1 egg white (optional)

Add all the ingredients to a cocktail shaker. Add ice and shake hard. Strain over ice into an Old Fashioned glass. Garnish with a twist of lemon. Serve.

Penicillin

Not widely known but thoroughly enjoyed by those who know it. It's a bit like having a cold hot toddy! You can use ginger-honey syrup but we like the fiery ginger and fresh honey combination.

Line recommendation: Amber Line
- ◯ 50 ml whisky
- ◯ 25 ml lemon juice
- ◯ 2 tsp honey
- ◯ 3 slices fresh ginger

Muddle fresh ginger and add with all the ingredients to a cocktail shaker. Add ice and shake hard. Strain over ice into an Old Fashioned glass. Garnish with a twist of lemon. Serve.

Hot Toddy

The perfect winter cold/flu cure-all and much more enjoyable than a Lemsip.

Line recommendation: Easy Loop
- ◯ 50 ml whisky
- ◯ 25 ml lemon juice
- ◯ 1 tsp honey
- ◯ Cinnamon stick or cloves (optional)
- ◯ Boiling water

Pour honey into an Irish Coffee mug. Add other ingredients. Top up with boiling water. Garnish with cinnamon stick and lemon slice. Serve.

Buying, storing and investing

Googling buying, storing or investing in whisky can result in a confusing jumble of advice, false information and general confusion. It doesn't need to be like that though. Not if you have common sense and an eye for a bargain.

Where to buy whisky

Whisky is readily available in all sort of places, including off-licences, corner shops, wine shops, supermarkets and specialist whisky shops. Most of the whiskies on the WhiskyTubeMap will be found in at least one of that list, and many will be in a number of them.

Check out the whisky section next time you are in your local supermarket for any special deals or offers, as they often stock a wide range of whiskies, not just the most obvious ones. Most supermarkets also bottle their own label blended whisky and sometimes single malt whiskies. These are generally of a decent quality and much cheaper than buying brand name whiskies. The only downside is that even though the whiskies are often made by well-known whisky distilleries it won't say where the whisky is from, it might simply say something like: Glen-Supermarket Speyside single malt. It's good to have a look at a review or to try one at a consumer fair first if you can, as they can sometimes be a bit hit or miss.

A whisky specialist shop is the best place to head if you want to get some advice. They are particularly good if you are looking for something specific or need advice about what to buy, perhaps for a gift or if you are looking to find a whisky from one of the WhiskyTubeMap stations.

Sadly, not every town has a good whisky shop, but you would be surprised how many wine shops tend to stock a broad range of whiskies. They may have some interesting independent bottlings or hard-to-find bottles, and be able to give you some good advice.

If you don't have a good local source, or can't find what you are looking for nearby, you can get access to an ever-increasing range of whisky online, assuming you are happy to wait a couple days for delivery. It is often more competitively priced, as online retailers have fewer overheads than traditional whisky specialist shops, although you should always check out their credentials before you buy.

There are an ever-increasing number of online whisky retailers; two 'go-to's are *www.masterofmalt.com* and *www.thewhiskyexchange.com*. Both have international shipping as well as next-day delivery available, and exemplary customer service.

What to pay for your whisky

The price of whisky can vary dramatically depending on the distillery, how rare it is, how old it is and who is selling it, to name just a few of the factors. If you're splashing out on a bottle it is worth doing a bit of homework to find the best source, as it may not be where you would expect. It is worth noting that a lot of the things that affect price aren't actually about the quality itself, and you don't have to spend a fortune to get a good whisky. Whisky pricing seems to be in an upward trajectory at the moment. There appears to be no rhyme or reason behind pricing; for example, you could pay £50 for a 16-year-old single malt or a 3-year-old whisky from a brand new distillery, a blended whisky or a non-age statement whisky. But a lot of this is about trend, novelty and appearances and not about quality; you don't have to pay a fortune to drink good whisky.

The distillery

Just like fashion, the name of the distillery will have a bearing on cost – some distilleries have a bigger price tag. It's important to know that sometimes you're paying for the cachet of the name.

The rareness and age

Some whiskies are made in smaller batches or from a single cask; if fewer bottles are produced, the cost goes up proportionally. And as more bottles are consumed, there are fewer bottles left, so the price goes up even more. Older whiskies are generally rarer, so that pushes the price up too.

The independent bottler

You can often get very good value for money by buying whiskies bottled by an independent bottler. Independent bottlers buy casks from distilleries and bottle them themselves. Because you are not buying the whisky from the distillery itself, known as an 'own bottling', you can sometimes get a real bargain. Keep an eye open for independent bottlings from the Scotch Malt Whisky Society, Wemyss Malts and Douglas Laing, just to name a few.

The seller

Most of the bigger brands try to have standardised pricing of their whiskies but inevitably the retailer can decide how much they charge, often based on their operating costs. It's always worth doing a little bit of comparison when you are trying out a new shop or website to see how much they charge for widely available products, which should give you a steer for their mark-ups of other products. If they are expensive for well-known brands and distilleries, they are likely to be expensive for other whiskies.

How to store whisky

Happily, it is much easier to store whisky than it is to store wine.

Unlike wine, whisky does not age in the bottle. It doesn't age or change (too much) once opened either. If you keep a 10-year-old whisky for 100 years before opening it, it will still be a 10-year-old whisky when you drink it.

To keep your whisky in prime condition:
O *Never* store whisky on its side (horizontally) like wine. *Always* store it upright (vertically).
   O The high alcohol level of whisky could cause the cork to deteriorate if it is on its side, causing evaporation, or the cork to crumble into the whisky.
O Keep your whisky somewhere with a constant temperature, so not your airing cupboard. Not too hot and not too humid (nothing hotter than an unheated room) to minimise the chance of evaporation.
O Keep your whisky out of direct sunlight. The best place is a completely cool, dark place like a cellar.
   O Ultraviolet radiation from direct sunlight could have a detrimental effect on whisky over time, particularly those in clear bottles.

How to store opened bottles
Once a whisky has been opened it will very gradually start to oxidise. However, unlike wine, this will take a long time and is much more subtle to detect. Generally speaking, once a whisky has been opened it should taste at its best for up to two years. However, the amount of oxidation that occurs will very much depend on the amount of air in the neck of the bottle. The more whisky you drink the more air there will be in the bottle. But in all seriousness, don't worry about this too much unless you are drinking very expensive or very old bottles of whisky.

Geek tips – if you are particularly precious about your whisky:
O Use inert gas, such as nitrogen, to seal-fill the neck of the bottle before putting the cork in. The nitrogen is heavier

than oxygen so creates a barrier between the whisky and the air outside the bottle.

O Use parafilm (or similar) to seal the cork. Wrap one piece over the bottle stopper and then wrap a second piece around the neck, in the style of a tennis racket grip, to seal the first piece.

O Decant smaller amounts (less than half a bottle) of special whiskies into smaller bottles to reduce the chance of oxidation if they aren't frequently used.

How to store unopened bottles

Remembering the key fundamentals of storing upright, at a cool temperature and out of sunlight, your whisky should last for a long time with no negative effects or evaporation

Geek tips – if you are particularly precious about your whisky and you are planning on keeping bottles for several years before opening:

O Use parafilm (or similar) to seal the cork. Wrap one piece over the bottle stopper and then wrap a second piece around the neck, in the style of a tennis racket grip, to seal the first piece.

O Store in a cool, dark place.

Investing in whisky

The WhiskyTubeMap has been designed with whisky drinkers in mind rather than whisky for collection or investment. But it is a hot topic at the moment, and the whisky auction market has been booming in the last five or so years. There are now several specialist online whisky auction websites as well as the traditional auction house with annual whisky sales. This has also led to a rise in so-called 'Investment Grade Scotch'. This has, for some, been showing better return on investment than gold. Whisky investment and collecting is a huge topic in itself, but something to remember is that when the whisky was made, it

was made to be enjoyed, not to gather dust on a shelf somewhere as a trophy item. One technique that many whisky investors use is to buy two bottles of a whisky, that way they can drink one and keep one. Or end up drinking the second one if they enjoyed it so much.

Like any investment, the price of the whisky could go down depending on the market. However, unlike shares or other investments, at least you can drink it if the price does crash.

A few simple key points to bear in mind if you are planning to start investing in whisky:

- Whisky brand name and distillery are very important.
  - Certain brands perform much better than others, especially whisky from closed distilleries.
- Rare or limited editions.
  - The rarer the whisky the better, especially discontinued expressions or bottlings no longer available.
- Use common sense and watch out for fakes.
  - There is a lot of fake and counterfeit whisky out there so be careful. If it seems too good to be true, it probably is.

Public service announcement

How to spot a fake:

- Any strange typos on the label.
- A declared abv of less than 40 per cent (which is the legal minimum).
- The age statement on the bottle is less than three years (again, this is the legal minimum).
- It says it is a Scotch whisky but wasn't made in Scotland (most fakes are of Scotch whiskies).

If you do notice a whisky with any of the above you should contact the Legal Affairs Department at the Scotch Whisky Association. At any one time they have up to seventy legal cases going on around the world, defending Scotch whisky and eliminating fakes and counterfeits from the market.

Troubleshooting

It is very rare to experience a problem with a bottle of whisky, mostly due to modern improvements in the production and bottling of whisky. However, if you do think something is wrong with your whisky then you should return it, with the receipt, to the shop where you bought it. If you have been served a whisky in a bar or restaurant and think there is something wrong with it you should tell the waiter or bartender and, if necessary, be prepared to stand your ground.

The symptoms	The fault	The solution
My whisky has gone hazy/cloudy.	This happens to non-chill-filtered (NCF) whisky when it gets cold. Note: this also happens when you add water to NCF whisky.	☺ Keep it. This happens if a bottle gets cold. Move the bottle somewhere warmer and the haze will go away as it adjusts to room temperature.
The cork snapped when I opened it.	Dry or old cork.	☺ Use a corkscrew. Carefully extract the cork and pick out any bits, or use a tea strainer when pouring.
Glass or other foreign bodies.	Clearly this should not happen and could be dangerous.	☹ Send it back. Try to take all the packaging (cork/screwcap) back with the bottle.

FAQ / Mythbusting

Whisky has a lot of urban myths and hearsay attached to it, much of which just isn't true ...

Question	Answer
My whisky looks very light in colour, is there something wrong with it?	Whiskies vary in colour depending on the cask they were matured in. Just because a whisky is light in colour doesn't mean there is anything wrong with it. See p. 15.
Is darker whisky better?	Not necessarily. Some large whisky producers use caramel colouring (E150a) to create a consistency of colour, or for certain markets may make a whisky darker in colour because of this preconception. See p. 15.
Is older whisky better?	Not necessarily. See p. 15.
Is expensive whisky better?	Not necessarily. It's all about your own preferences and the right whisky at the right time.
This whisky doesn't have an age on it. Why is this?	This is referred to as a Non-Age Statement whisky. This means the whisky can be any age (over three years old). Don't let this put you off though, a Non-Age Statement gives the distillery more options to create exactly the whisky they want to.

Question	Answer
How long can I leave a bottle of whisky open?	As long as you like. However, the more air there is in the neck of the bottle, the more the whisky could oxidise. See p. 130 for more details about whisky storage.
Does a whisky age in the bottle like wine?	A ten-year-old whisky will still be ten years old even if you keep it for 100 years before opening it. See p. 130 for more details about whisky storage.
How do you say 'cheers' in Scots?	Slàinte Mhath (pronounced 'Slan-Je-Var')

Advanced manoeuvres

Congratulations, you've read the book, you've discovered new favourites and tested your taste buds in different ways. The whisky 'bug' has bitten you and you are now presumably looking for what to do next.

Host a whisky party

Get some of your friends round, make sure to invite those who also don't like whisky (so you can convert them). One of the best ways to learn more about whisky is to taste two or three whiskies side by side, you will then literally be able to taste the differences.

O Pick a section of the WhiskyTubeMap and three to six whiskies from it.

O Ask your friends to bring a different whisky each from the stations you have selected – make sure to set a budget so it is fair for everyone.

O Pour a sample of each whisky into a different glass, put a sticker on each glass with a number (if doing it 'blind') or the name of the whisky on it.

O Try the whiskies in the same order as in the WhiskyTubeMap and note the differences you detect – which ones you like, don't like and why.

O Pick your favourite whisky and have a larger dram of it with some cheeses or chocolates (see Food on p. 119 for more ideas) and over the evening put the world to rights.

O Why not make it a regular thing with your whisky-loving friends? It's a great way to explore the WhiskyTubeMap and learn more about whisky.

Go for a WhiskyTubeMap journey at a whisky bar

Perhaps you happen to be visiting a city with a particularly good whisky bar or perhaps you live near a bar with a broad whisky selection. This is a great way to discover more about whisky: think of it as a kind of try-before-you-buy. After trying a dram of something in a bar, knowing that you liked it means you can buy a full-size bottle without the risk of not enjoying it.

- O Take your copy of WhiskyTubeMap with you.
- O Choose a 'journey' of between three and six whiskies.
- O Ask for them to be served at the same time so you can compare them side by side.
- O Taste them in the same order as on the WhiskyTubeMap to see what the differences are.
- O Set a budget (in your mind) before you go or you could end up getting carried away.

Plan your whisky journey

Once you've tried all the whiskies around the favourites that you've known and loved for a long time, plot a more adventurous route and over time work your way through it. Keep an eye out for these whiskies going on promotion, or buy them when there is a deal or offer on them. It's a great way to build up your repertoire and your home bar.

Glossary

Like most specialist subjects, whisky has its own unique jargon. Common and geeky expressions and terminology used in *The Pocket Guide to Whisky* are below:

Age Statement The age of the whisky, stated on the label. Note: this is the age of the youngest whisky in the bottle. For example, a 10-year-old whisky could also contain 12-year-old whisky, but the label can only state 10.

Alcohol by volume (abv) The standard measure of how much alcohol is in an alcoholic drink, expressed as a percentage.

Angels' share The alcohol that evaporates during the maturation process. Normally around 2 per cent volume per annum in Scotland, but it can be significantly higher in hotter whisky-producing countries.

Blended whisky Whisky made from a combination of single malt whisky and single grain whisky.

Blended malt whisky A blend of solely single malt whiskies.

Bourbon Whisky made in America from at least 51 per cent maize (corn) and matured in new charred oak barrels.

Cask strength Whisky bottled at the same strength as when it came out of the cask. In normal practice whisky is reduced to 40 per cent abv (legal minimum) at the time of bottling.

Chill-filtration Chill-filtration removes congeners from the whisky that would cause it to go foggy/hazy at cold temperatures. Many specialist whiskies are non-chill-filtered (NCF).

Continuous distillation A much cheaper and more efficient process of distilling compared to batch distillation in copper pot stills. Single grain whisky is distilled using continuous distillation.

Expression/bottling Expression or bottling is the term used in the whisky world to describe a specific batch or whisky made by a distillery. This could be a one-off limited edition or a core product in their portfolio, like Glenmorangie 10-year-old.

Distillation The process of heating a wash to the point of evaporation when it then condenses into a purer alcohol.

Finishing When a whisky is transferred to a different type of cask to 'finish' the maturation. Usually only for a short period of time.

Floor maltings The traditional process of malting barley, where barley is spread out on a large floor and turned by hand. Mostly superseded by industrial malting.

Green malt Barley that has not been completely dried in the malting process.

Independent bottling (IB) A bottling by an independent bottler who has purchased a cask from a distillery and bottled it themselves.

Malted barley Barley that has been allowed to partially germinate, which is then heated to stop the germination.

Mash The porridge-like mixture of ground malted barley and hot water.

Mothballed When a distillery stops producing whisky but is kept in good condition in case the distillery reopens.

New make spirit The name for the liquid that comes off the still during the distillation process, before it is put into casks to mature.

Non-chill-filtered (NCF) See chill-filtration.

Own bottling (OB) A bottling produced by a brand or distillery.

Peat Partly decomposed vegetable matter which when burnt gives off a pungent smoke, used during the malting process to make peated whiskies. Peat was the traditional source of fuel used by crofters, because it was readily available.

Pot still A copper pot still used for batch distillation. Generally distilled twice.

Parts per million (PPM) of phenols The measurement for phenols (or smokiness) of a whisky.

Reflux Vapour in the distillation process that drops back down and is effectively re-distilled.

Single cask whisky Whisky bottled from a single cask in order to create a unique and limited edition.

Single grain whisky Whisky distilled in the continuous distillation method from maize (corn) or wheat.

Single malt whisky Whisky made from malted barley at a single distillery.

Wash The alcoholic beer-like liquid that is distilled to make whisky.

Worm tubs Coils of copper pipe, in large vats of water, which help the condensation of vapours during distillation.

General index

Additional whiskies index

Not all whiskies or distilleries can be featured on the WhiskyTubeMap itself but they do fit in the bigger picture. This list gives you an indication of which line some other whiskies and distilleries fit on.

Acknowledgements

This has been a hugely collaborative process and we would like to thank Kirstie Paton from Go! Bang! Creative Ltd for her work on the visuals, for bringing the map to life and for creating a fabulous colour palette. And Steve Cooney, who very kindly helped us out when we were researching the flavour lines.

We both brought very different things to this process, which means we've got some individual thanks.

From Blair

The WhiskyTubeMap would not exist without many people who have been incredibly generous to me over the years with their time, knowledge and experience. Without them I would not have had the 'lie of the land' to bring to this process. For every tasting, distillery visit or chat over a dram, thank you! I would also like to thank my lovely wife and my parents for their never-ending love and support, without whom I would not have been able to write this book.

From Nikki

A huge thanks to the team at Birlinn for believing in the concept and for the nudge to create the next map. The original inspiration came from Ged, who I must also thank for the epic whisky tastings and inspired ideas at crucial moments. And to the many people who have given me their feedback on the WineTubeMap™ over the years; it has proved invaluable in this process. Don't stop now!

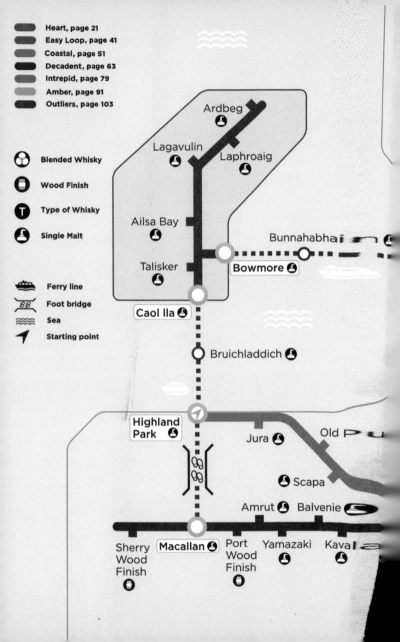

Blended Whisky

Wood Finish

Type of Whisky

Single Malt

Ferry line

Foot bridge

Sea

Starting point

Ardbeg

Lagavulin

Laphroaig

Ailsa Bay

Bunnahabhain

Talisker

Bowmore

Caol Ila

Bruichladdich

Highland Park

Jura

Old Pu

Scapa

Amrut

Balvenie

Macallan

Sherry Wood Finish

Port Wood Finish

Yamazaki

Kaval